America in Bloom

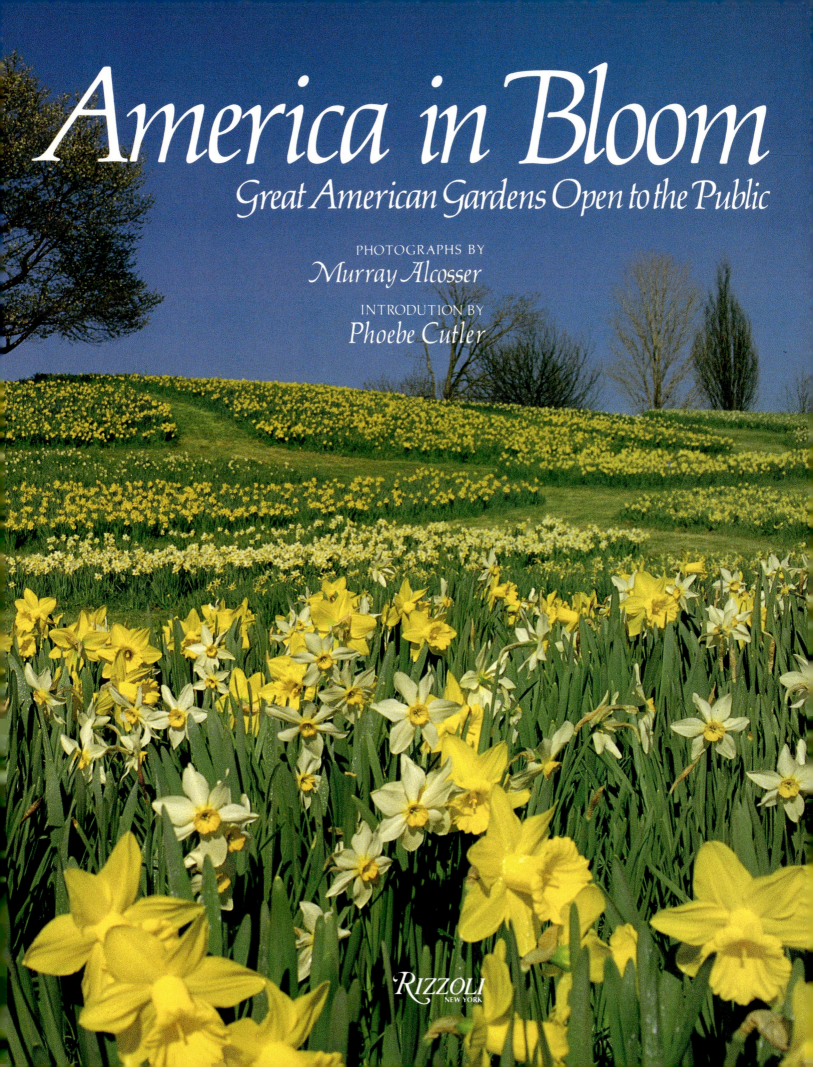

America in Bloom

Great American Gardens Open to the Public

PHOTOGRAPHS BY
Murray Alcosser

INTRODUCTION BY
Phoebe Cutler

RIZZOLI
NEW YORK

For Lily

First published in the United States of America in 1991 by
Rizzoli International Publications, Inc.
300 Park Avenue South, New York, New York 10010

Copyright © 1991 Rizzoli International Publications, Inc.
All rights reserved. No part of this publication may be reproduced in any manner
whatsoever without permission in writing from Rizzoli International Publications.

Library of Congress Cataloging-in-Publication Data
Alcosser, Murray, 1937-
    America in bloom: great American gardens open to the public/
photographs by Murray Alcosser: introduction by Phoebe Cutler.
    Includes index.
    ISBN 0-8478-1326-6
    1. Gardens—United States—Pictorial works.   2. Gardens—United
States.   3. Photography of gardens.   4. United States—Description
and travel—1981- —Views.   I. Title.
SB466.U6A34   1991   90-50798
712'.0973—dc20   CIP

Frontispieces:
Page 1: Longwood Gardens, Kennett Square, Pennsylvania; Pages 2-3: Winterthur,
Winterthur, Delaware; Page 6: Virginia Robinson Gardens, Beverly Hills, California;
Page 15: Dumbarton Oaks, Washington, D.C.

Design by Charles Davey
Garden descriptions by Marjorie Merrow, Jean Quayle, and Glenn Johnston
Typeset by Graphic Arts Composition, Philadelphia
Printed and bound in Tokyo by Dai Nippon Printing Company

CONTENTS

7 Introduction
by Phoebe Cutler

16 Rose Garden,
Woodland Park
Seattle, Washington

20 Japanese Tea Garden,
Washington Park Arboretum
Seattle, Washington

22 Filoli
Woodside, California

28 Hearst Castle
San Simeon, California

32 Virginia Robinson Gardens
Beverly Hills, California

36 Santa Barbara Botanic Garden
Santa Barbara, California

42 J. Paul Getty Museum
Malibu, California

48 Descanso Gardens
La Canada, California

52 Los Angeles State and
County Arboretum
Arcadia, California

58 The Huntington
San Marino, California

66 Balboa Park
San Diego, California

72 Quail Botanical Gardens
Encinitas, California

74 Dallas Arboretum
and Botanical Garden
Dallas, Texas

86 Fort Worth Botanic Garden
Fort Worth, Texas

92 Chicago Botanic Garden
Glencoe, Illinois

98 Lincoln Park
Chicago, Illinois

100 Garfield Park
Chicago, Illinois

102 Grant Park
Chicago, Illinois

104 Longue Vue
New Orleans, Louisiana

110 City Park
New Orleans, Louisiana

114 Vizcaya
Miami, Florida

120 Fairchild Tropical Garden
Miami, Florida

124 Four Arts Garden
Palm Beach, Florida

128 Callaway Gardens
Pine Mountain, Georgia

132 Atlanta Botanical Garden
Atlanta, Georgia

136 Magnolia Plantation
Charleston, South Carolina

142 Middleton Place
Charleston, South Carolina

148 Monticello
Charlottesville, Virginia

154 Dumbarton Oaks
Washington, D.C.

162 Winterthur
Winterthur, Delaware

168 Nemours
Wilmington, Delaware

174 Longwood Gardens
Kennett Square, Pennsylvania

184 The Cloisters
New York, New York

188 Brooklyn Botanic Garden
Brooklyn, New York

194 New York Botanical Garden
Bronx, New York

200 Wave Hill
Bronx, New York

206 Old Westbury Gardens
Old Westbury, New York

214 Isabella Stewart
Gardner Museum
Boston, Massachusetts

218 Acknowledgments

219 Public Garden Source List

223 Index

Introduction
by PHOEBE CUTLER

In 1741 an English landscape designer named Simms stood awed before a tranquil bend in the Ashley River. Before him lay a broad sweep of marshes teeming with wildlife and the gnarled silhouettes of giant oaks draped with Spanish moss. Faced with a landscape unlike anything he knew in Europe, this recently identified artist created a garden inspired by his homeland, but imbued with a freshness that must have sprung from a sense of freedom and wonder before the grandiloquence of America. For this Carolina Low Country plantation Simms balanced geometrically patterned gardens, or parterres, with a set of terraces descending from the house in the fashionable Italianate manner. Terraces like these, however, no Roman or Florentine had ever trod. No double stairways or balustraded walls impede their broad sweep. Their expanse is greater than any of the known British precedents. They angle and curve, break and reform in their progress to meet the marsh land to the north, the pond to the south, and the Ashley on the east. Their freedom celebrates the freedom of a new land—America in bloom.

While the turfed steps evoke seventeenth- and early eighteenth-century British variations on Italian design, the layout of parterres, the former Mount, and the Reflecting Pool of South Carolina's Middleton Place demonstrate an eighteenth-century Parisian precision that comes right out of a French garden primer of the day, written by Dezallier d'Argenville. A right triangle laid over the plan of the garden elements peaks in an axis running through the terraces and the twin Butterfly Lakes. The different parts of the composition merge together to focus on the landscape-at-large.

In Thomas Jefferson's eyes Middleton Place would have been a little passé, a little too dernière siècle. In 1786 Jefferson, accompanied by John Adams, went on a tour of English country homes to prepare himself for the designing of the garden of his Virginia home Monticello. He was able to experience first-hand the gardening revolution that had ushered out the parterre and the stepped terrace and brought in the undulating meadow and scattered groves of trees—a landscape that stylized the pastoral scene browsed into being by rural England's herds of sheep and cattle. The torpid Southern climate had foiled Jefferson's pioneering efforts to introduce the English or "natural" style of landscaping. The random arrangement of trees did not provide enough protection against the glaring Virginia sun, so Jeffer-

son, in conformity to the theme of compromise and adaptability presented above, was forced to alter a European precedent. He planted the trees close together, but pruned them up high in order to achieve a sense of openness. For the random effect he had to content himself with scattering clumps of shrubs beneath the protective canopy he had created. With this improvised "Grove" and with the flowing lawn that comprised the West Front, Jefferson set himself squarely on the side of the natural school that was to dominate much of nineteenth-century park and residential design and continues as a force into this century.

Middleton Place and Monticello both introduce a theme that runs throughout American landscape architecture. The need to define a garden in relationship to Europe has consistently influenced the shaping of the land. Three different views towards Europe came into play in the making of these two Southern plantations. Henry Middleton, owner of Middleton Place, took the combative approach, expressly trying to outdo the mother country at her own art. His designer found creative inspiration in the foreign situation , subordinating his own vision to the drama of the natural setting. For his part, Jefferson sought valiantly and ironically to stay au courant *with England, a country from which ten years earlier he had demanded political separation. Jefferson is a poignant case in this volatile relationship of parent and child, benefactor and beneficee that continues to the Post-Modern classic revival of our own day. The most enduring compositions, like Monticello and Middleton Place, manage to commingle the strains of old and new to create gardens of resonance and beauty.*

Others, not long after Thomas Jefferson's mixed success at Monticello, took up the cause for the English school of landscaping. Andrew Jackson Downing became its chief spokesman, while Frederick Law Olmsted was its principal protagonist. Olmsted's early and great interpretations of both the pastoral and the picturesque branches of the British style of landscaping were so successful that all succeeding American interpretations of the great English gardens at Blenheim, Stowe, and Longleat, descend through Central Park and Boston's Fens. All the gardens of any size in this book are in some part, if not in their totality, indebted to the achievement of Olmsted and the firm he founded.

The results of Chicago's contracting for a park system from 1870 through the 1890s give ample proof of the influence that the British Isles and Olmsted Brothers exerted, and still exert, over this country's soil. Olmsted, reacting probably very much like Simms looking over the Ashley 130 years before, pronounced that the proposed Chicago sites weren't much—but the setting was superb. He pro-

claimed that the grandeur of the adjoining Lake Michigan compensated for the inadequacies of the flat boggy land. Then, like the designer of Middleton Place, he began to mold the ground. He dug out lagoons and lakes and with the fill created gently undulating land. Then he called, albeit unsuccessfully, for thick copses to line the shore and cast their reflection onto a Lake Michigan tranquilized by weirs. Although he declaimed that no man-made rise could improve upon the spectacle of the lake, Olmsted could not rid himself of the hills of his East Coast upbringing and his English inclination. The setting of ponds, swells, shrubs, and trees that characterize Lincoln, Jackson, and Washington Parks was not one a Midwestern gopher would recognize. The prairie would have to wait another twenty years for its champion.

Although the prairie mode was not one of them, American landscape architecture firms of the nineteenth and early twentieth centuries were by necessity adept at working in more than one style. As foreshadowed by the dual strains of parterre and grass terraces at Middleton Place, the United States was heir to too many heritages to be content with only one methodology. Moreover, contrasting needs required different treatments. Use of the informal often invoked a counter need for its opposite. Indeed, in his master plan for Chicago, Daniel Burnham had set aside a focal area on Michigan Avenue near the mouth of the Chicago River to be the centerpiece of the South Park system. For such spaces, nineteenth-century America turned to the example of France. Given the commission to design this park, the Olmsted firm organized it with mirror-image planting beds and matching radial paths straight out of the Tuileries and 1870 Beaux-Arts Paris. Today floral displays persist, although the ground plan has been much simplified since the 1920s plan and the area has been hemmed in by highways. Still, however, the mighty, bowl-shaped Buckingham Fountain adorns its midpoint.

The Buckingham Fountain evokes Paris and the Second Empire, but a different set of smaller, slimmer fountain bowls that began to appear across the land at the turn of the century evidenced a third influence that eventually outdid the example of France and complemented the paradigm of England. Several of these less grandiose bowls appeared as planters on the terrace of the house of what is known today as Old Westbury Gardens. Another adorned the top of the cascade at Vizcaya, a winter retreat built in 1917 in Miami. Whether borrowed from one of the fountains in Rome's Borghese gardens, or from the chalice at the head of the water ramp at the Villa Farnese in Caprarola, or from the Isolotto of the Boboli Garden in Florence, these bowls symbolize an era when all drafting tables, veering away from France, pointed towards Italy. France was not ignored and other countries, particularly Spain and Japan, made their contribution to an unprec-

edented era—1890 to 1930—of great house and garden building, but the biggest donor by far was Italy. Designers—Charles Platt, Beatrice Farrand, James Greenleaf, and Herbert Hare, to name a few; industrialists—J. P. Morgan, Pierre du Pont, James Freer, and more—scoured the Appenines for their inspiration. When the Chicago novelist, Henry B. Fuller published Waldo Trench and Others *in 1908, the hero of one of the short stories was honeymooning in Florence while directing via letter the construction of his Italianate garden in Long Island. For fifty years Italy's pergolas, balustrades, pools, and fountains shaped North America's most prized outdoor spaces.*

As a result of this fervor of discovery of the gardens of sixteenth- and seventeenth-century Italy, Americans blithefully mixed eras, styles, and nations in compositions ranging from public rose garden amphitheaters to private terraced cascades. James Deering's Vizcaya outdid all other estates in its carefree assemblage of disparate garden parts. The few acres of this garden regale the visitor with a Roman cascade, a pavilion from the vicinity of Rome, an island like one in the Tiber, a Sienese theater garden, a Venetian bridge, and French parterres in the manner of Versailles. In comparison, William Randolph Hearst's efforts at San Simeon seem restrained. There an Imperial Roman pool and a Renaissance Italian guesthouse are subordinate to an overall Spanish tone. Whether the flavor was Spanish, as at San Simeon, or French, as at Longwood and Nemours, the fountains, statuary, the long axial vistas, and tiered descents trace their eventual ancestry to the hills of Florence and Rome.

The normal procedure for the design of the grounds of a country estate in its golden era of 1880 to 1930 usually entailed the use of the English or informal style as the framework into which a sunken garden, an allée, a cascade, a rose garden, and, very often, a Japanese garden, would be inserted. Old Westbury, Wave Hill, and Winterthur are exemplary East Coast representatives of this approach; while the original DeGolyer gardens of the Dallas Arboretum, the Virginia Robinson Gardens, the Huntington, and Filoli illustrate the western equivalent. A master of the technique, such as Beatrice Farrand, could blend a cassoulet of Old World elements and come up with a subtle and unified composition enlivened by wisteria, forsythia, and crab apple.

Beatrice Farrand's designs were not always so subtle. Dumbarton Oaks, in Washington D.C., developed over a period of twenty years, represents the culmination of this landscape architect's career. It also symbolizes a plateau in the evolution of American imitation of European prototypes. The earlier tycoon statements of the first couple of decades, like Vizcaya and Longwood, proudly proclaimed their debt.

Vizcaya's Casino is an obvious remake of the pavilion from the upper garden of the Villa Farnese at Caprarola; while Pierre du Pont's water wall clearly emerged from the Villa d'Este. The recognizability of the sources was desirable, lending authentication to the garden.

By the thirties and forties—the era of the DeGolyer gardens in Dallas, the Callaway Gardens near Columbus, Georgia; Longue Vue in New Orleans, and the final phase of Dumbarton Oaks, the excesses of the Prohibition years and the Jazz Age were a faintly incredulous memory for people living in a much soberer time. The Great Depression and the Dust Bowl separated the 350 acres of Longwood with its 800-odd fountain heads and the eight acres of, the admittedly urban, Longue Vue with its yellow-flowering patio and Louisiana sugar-kettle-turned-reflecting-pool. Designers and clients moved with greater ease in and out and all around the European garden heritage, made familiar by one more generation of exposure and by the availability of an abundance of publications. As seen by the Arbor Terrace and amphitheater of Dumbarton Oaks, Americans were still using the classic formats, but more as a point of departure and less as a model to aspire to.

Americans had become more relaxed about Europe and, correspondingly, more accepting of their own heritage. As early as 1906, the prairie had found a landscape champion. As superintendent and planner for Chicago's West Park System, Jens Jensen introduced a prairie river into Columbus Park. At Garfield he built a giant conservatory and filled it, not with South American palms and East Asian orchids, but with mock-ups of prairie habitats. Subsequently, in his residential plans for the Midwestern elite, Jensen substituted Indian council rings for the Italian garden amphitheater and red buds and witch hazel for boxwood and arborvitae. Although determinedly individualistic, Jensen was not alone in his call for flowing forms and indigenous planting.

In 1930 while Jensen was writing to his client Edsel Ford to advise him on the virtue of change in a maturing landscape, in a very different part of the country, but with a not dissimilar vision, Cason and Virginia Callaway began rehabilitating a twenty-five-hundred-acre valley in western Georgia. Partially spurred on by the discovery of a rare and threatened azalea unique to the area, the Callaways sought to return worn-out cotton-growing land to the rich forest community that had existed there before. They ended up with that forest, and also a golf course, thirteen lakes, lodgings, and restaurants before they were done, but the glory of the Callaway Gardens has always been and still is its immense panoply of Southern plantings in a luxuriant, naturalistic manner that is far removed from the parterres of the teens and twenties.

The Callaways were doing on a private and more elaborate scale what the New Deal was simultaneously carrying out in state and national parks and forests all over the country. A nation-wide drive for conservation and a movement for expanded recreational facilities joined forces during the thirties. Employing the thousands thrown out of work by the Depression, government organizations intent upon both causes made an indelible mark on the land. By the end of the decade the number of state parks had increased by nearly a third; New York City had tripled its stock of playgrounds, and national parks and forests had greatly multiplied their roads, structures, campgrounds, and trails. Along with parks, botanic gardens benefitted appreciably from the federal subsidies of the New Deal. At least three of the botanical gardens in this volume exhibit the tell-tale sign that the Works Progress Administration, its precursor the Civil Works Administration, or the Civilian Conservation Corps were once at work here. The Forth Worth Botanical Garden, the University of Washington Arboretum, and the Fairchild Tropical Gardens at opposite ends of the nation all contain examples of the hand-made stone work that more than anything betrays the Depression origins of a place.

The rose garden in the Fort Worth Botanical Garden is the quintessential New Deal garden. The rose has always been the national favorite among flowers, but never more than during the thirties. The economic collapse of the period largely halted the spending that in historically unprecedented amounts had been lavished on private home-building in the forty years prior. (William Randolph Hearst enlarged one pool and added another between 1927 and 1936 and the Blisses kept going at Dumbarton Oaks; otherwise the private gardens connected with houses included in this book were constructed either before 1929 or begun after 1939.) The moguls' losses became the public's gain. The rose gardens, cascades, garden theaters, and tennis courts that had been part and parcel of the rich man's estate were now resurrected in parks all over the country. Fort Worth, for example, hired the landscape architects Hare and Hare who had just finished three years earlier an Italian cascade à la Caprarola for the Waite Phillipses' in Tulsa. In the best thirties' fashion Hare and Hare brought to Fort Worth the same form of a terraced garden with a water chain running through the middle; only this time the water ran through roses not boxwood and the material was local field rock, not Mankato limestone imported from Minnesota. Through the agency of the Civil Works Administration, a Renaissance cardinal's and Oklahoma oil baron's extravagance blossomed as a public garden on the North Texas plains.

An Italianate rose garden arising on the Texas prairie implies that Americans in the thirties were continuing to import the principal forms of their landscape pleasures. So far, among other extravagances, the delight in the exotic had brought the Gardner Museum, a Venetian palazzo, to Boston in 1902, a Medieval cloister to New York in 1938, and a Japanese garden to Brooklyn. Whether on or off the prairie, Jens Jensen's message was being ignored.

The founding of the Santa Barbara Botanic Garden in 1926, however, indicated signs that support for the native landscape was building in places other than Chicago. This mountain-side garden stated as its purpose the preservation and display of California's native flora. Subsequent generous space allocations in the Coast's numerous botanic gardens—Descanso, Quail, and the Los Angeles County Arboretum among them—the native plant movement caught fire. Alighting the rest of the country, it culminated in the seventies. Chicago, ever loyal to its heroes, in 1965, opened up a botanical garden in a marsh that both preserved the marsh and highlighted native species.

The revolt of the sixties and seventies involved more than just planting lists. The traditional Italian and English designs, thrown off their pinnacle by the Modernist movement of the fifties, were dragged down deeper by Ian McHarg and his tract Design with Nature. *Emphasizing a scientific rationale to design, McHarg called for an understanding of soils and water conditions in an approach that went ten steps beyond the use of indigenous plants.*

Landscape architects dutifully busying themselves with soil studies and plant successions left their rear yards undefended and the site artists of the seventies stole up on them. Robert Smithson built his Spiral Jetty, *the eloquent land sculpture in the middle of the Great Salt Lake. Also conceived during this period of rebellion and professional cross-fertilization, the Dallas Botanical Garden came up with its "Worlds Counterparts" and "Moon" gardens—far from the perennial borders and Shakespeare gardens of Brooklyn and New York. The rupture with Europe looked almost complete.*

Nevertheless, the seventies also saw the opening of the Getty Museum and its archaeologically correct Roman garden. The Getty was still only a portent, but ensuing events, such as Charles Moore's Piazza d'Italia in New Orleans, confirmed that the Italian space was back. As in the past, the two strands—British and continental, informal and formal—coexisted again. With the revival of the Italian and French garden came the resuscitation of the English gardenesque work of Gertrude Jekyll and William Robinson. The perennial borders of the Italian Garden (now called the "Walled Garden") at Old Westbury gained new meaning. Robinson's and Jekyll's writing called for "wild gardens" of meadows and woods strewn with bulbs and other naturalized plants. American interpretations added billow-

ing grasses to the loose planting mixtures. Finally, to complete a confused picture of multiple revivals, the 1990 winner of the International Peace Garden to be built in Washington D.C. is a **broderie**, *a curvilinear parterre, depicting an olive branch. America is truly abloom every which way.*

With its encyclopedic tastes the garden fervor of the last decade has entailed the rise of an enthusiastic preservation movement, to the list of which the Virginia Robinson Gardens in Beverly Hills is a recent addition. Right now the gardens being preserved mainly date from the latter years of the golden era of the country estate. The Robinson estate, with its terraces, its pool and Italianate pool house, and its exotic plant collection, is a good, suburban version of the type. In the future, subjects for safeguarding will number suburban corporate headquarters and maybe theme parks, like Disney World, and perhaps even an earthbound space installation. America has bloomed in multiple ways that have yet to be chartered.

America in Bloom
Great American Gardens Open to the Public

Rose Garden, Woodland Park

Woodland Park
Seattle, Washington

Late in the nineteenth century Guy Phinney, a homesick—and rather eccentric—Englishman, determined to make himself a grand English-style country estate in northern America. Having made his fortune by building the first saw mill on Seattle's Lake Washington, Phinney settled on a vast tract of untamed land by Green Lake and cleared the property for a park with gardens, a boathouse, and bandstand; he even installed a private trolley car. Some years later the city bought the property for a civic park. An impressive zoo was designed for the park by the famed Olmsted brothers, and in 1924 a small, formal rose garden was opened to the public on the park grounds.

The rose plants thrived in the moist Seattle climate and the reputation of the small garden began to circulate. Eventually it was chosen as an All-American Rose Selection Site for testing of new rose varieties. The garden was expanded to meet its new responsibilities and is today a two-and-one-half-acre delight, filled with thousands of rose plants—bush roses, hybrid teas, climbers, miniatures, tree roses— laid out in formal style among pools, fountains, and unusual oriental cypresses.

Woodland Park's Rose Garden; an Oriental cypress at the left is pruned to maintain its unusual appearance

Following: Birdbath at the center of the Garden

Japanese Tea Garden, Washington Park Arboretum
Seattle, Washington

The Arboretum was designed in the 1930s by John Charles and Frederick Law Olmsted, Jr., sons of America's principal landscape architect, Frederick Law Olmsted. Their design is in the English—or "park"—style of landscaping, with sweeping lawns and rolling meadows, interspersed with clusters of trees and tranquil walkways. Located on the eastern edge of Seattle, off Lake Washington, the Park has lovely waterfront trails with views of the lake and mountains beyond.

The Japanese Tea Garden, added to the Park in the 1960s, is one of America's finest. Although the muted, contemplative atmosphere of Japanese gardens stands in stark contrast to the theatrical, colorful displays of western gardens, Japanese elements began to appear in western landscaping as early as the 1900s and are seen today throughout gardens of America. The Japanese garden of the Arboretum was designed in Japan by Juki Iida, and built in Seattle on three acres with boulders carried over from the nearby Cascade Mountains and plants native to Japan.

The Arboretum is managed by the University of Washington, the Tea Garden by the Seattle Department of Parks and Recreation.

The Tea Garden designed by Juki Iida

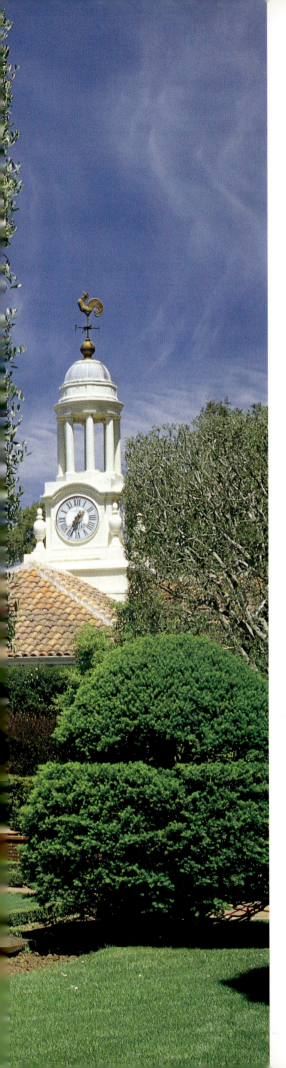

Filoli
Woodside, California

Filoli is regarded as one of the most beautifully designed gardens in the Western Hemisphere. Situated in redwood-covered hills, the 16-acre formal garden stands on a 654-acre estate bought early in this century as a home by Mr. and Mrs. William Bourn II, wealthy and prominent San Franciscans. Bourn created the name Filoli—an acronym for FIght, LOve, LIve—because the words embody a credo he admired: fight for a just cause, love your fellow men, live a good life.

The garden has been designed to take maximum advantage of its surroundings, resulting in a well-balanced blend of formal and natural elements. In addition to its clipped hedges, geometrically precise flowerbeds, yew-lined allée, artificial pools, and fountains, it contains collections of citrus and deciduous fruit trees, and groves of indigenous trees, including redwood and oak. A succession of separate areas or "rooms" has been created, each with its own distinctive character. A particularly striking "room"—and one that provides eloquent testimony to Bourn's expressed intention to create a garden resembling "horizontal stained glass"—is the Chartres Cathedral Garden. Here, a living replica of a stained glass window has been created in brilliantly colored flowers, with boxwood borders representing the window's lead outlines. Also unusual is the Knot Garden, a medieval invention created by branches of herb plantings interlaced so as to form intricate, visually arresting patterns—or "knots."

Other areas include: the Walled Garden, with an Italian Renaissance teahouse as its focal point; the Panel Garden, which contains a fruit orchard, with underplantings and borders comprising twenty-five thousand daffodils; the Woodland Garden, where a canopy of oaks filters sunlight over beds of azaleas, camellias, and rhododendrons; and the Rose Garden, with five-hundred bushes and over two-hundred varieties (Filoli is noted for its roses).

Filoli knows no seasonal restrictions. Plantings in all areas have been selected so as to create a floral display throughout the year. Mute testimony to its beauty is the inscription: "Time began in a garden."

A view of the Clock Tower from the Sunken Garden

Left: Chinese forget-me-nots outside the Rose Garden

Roses in front of a New Zealand tea tree in the Walled Garden

Foxglove in the Walled Garden

The Knot Garden

Left: *Joseph's coat roses in the Panel Garden*

The Sunken Garden with the Coast Range Mountains in the distance

The Sundial Garden planted with annuals

The Tea House pool

Hearst Castle
San Simeon, California

In 1919 William Randolph Hearst inherited from his miner-millionaire father 240,000 acres of California countryside, high above the Pacific. The land was a working cattle ranch half the size of the state of Rhode Island. Although he persisted in calling his property "the ranch," Hearst, together with the Beaux-Arts-trained architect Julia Morgan, proceeded to turn the bare California hills into a lush Mediterranean wonderland with, as its crowning glory, the hundred-room architectural extravaganza, Casa Grande. The Castle's rooms reflect a medley of styles from austere Gothic to sumptuous Spanish colonial. They include huge fireplaces, ceilings, even entire rooms transported from European castles and monasteries and painstakingly reassembled in the California hills.

To transform the surrounding countryside into a setting worthy of the grand, Mediterranean-inspired structure was a feat hardly less monumental than building the Casa itself. Millions of tons of topsoil were hauled up the hillside and the hill itself was sculpted into five terrace levels. Over one hundred thousand trees, an eclectic mix of palms, cypress, giant oaks, eucalyptus, Cedar of Lebanon, and redwood were transplanted to picturesque sites on the landscape. The hillsides were set ablaze with flowers—camellias, Hearst's own favorites, as well as fuchsias, azaleas, and star jasmine. Of the eighty-five landscaped acres of gardens and arboretum, five are formal gardens and include a rose garden with over fifty varieties of the rose. Five greenhouses supply the more than seven-hundred thousand annuals that are planted yearly. A mile-long pergola, or covered walk, is shaded by fruit trees and vines. Sculptures—some ancient, such as the thirty-five-hundred-year-old statue of an Egyptian goddess, others recent copies of famous works—have been placed around the gardens, as have pools and fountains. The most spectacular of these is the huge Neptune Pool, dominated at one end by the pedimented-and-columned-facade of a genuine Greco-Roman temple, flanked by elegantly curving colonnades.

In Hearst's day, a two-thousand-acre fenced-in park was home to some seventy species of wildlife—the largest private zoo in the world. Today, the more exotic animals are long since gone, but zebras, tahr goats, aoudad, and elk still roam the rolling hills of San Simeon.

Mexican fan palms appear to soar above Casa Grande's North Tower; roses are planted in the beds below

Madame Butterfly roses surrounding the Carrara marble statue, Girl with Kid

The Neptune Pool through the south colonnades

A statue of Europa surrounded by miniature roses

The courtyard of Casa del Monte, one of the estate's guest houses

Virginia Robinson Gardens
Beverly Hills, California

Early in this century, Harry and Virginia Robinson built their classic Mediterranean-revival house on a hillside north of Los Angeles. This was among the first of the lavish homes to grace Beverly Hills. The Robinsons diligently cultivated their six-acre property, turning the barren land—which was reputed to have fostered "only a single elderberry bush" at the time of the purchase—into a delightful array of terraced gardens, ponds, and fountains.

Linked by winding brick paths, the garden patios are exquisite year-round confections with displays of roses and flowering coral trees in the spring or summer and camellias and azaleas in the winter. A two-and-one-half-acre palm grove contains king palms. Behind the house, an expanse of lawn leads to the Renaissance-revival Pool House. Flowering oleanders cast their shadows over the pool beyond—among the first of the pools built in Beverly Hills.

Only recently opened to the public, the graceful blend of architectural whimsy and inspired landscaping make the Robinson Gardens one of the most intimate and charming of the numerous gardens along the country's West Coast. The Robinson's home is listed in the National Register of Historic Places; both the home and gardens are maintained by the Los Angeles County Department of Arboreta and Botanic Gardens.

A border of perennials—evening primrose, bush sage, Euryiops—along the walk to the Pool House

Left: Urn filled with asparagus overlooking the Rose Garden

A border of perennials with purple Mexican bush sage in the foreground

Italian cypress allée planted with verbena, poppies, and Joseph's coat roses

Balustrades and planted urns typify the Italianate style of the Gardens.

Santa Barbara Botanic Garden
Santa Barbara, California

The Santa Barbara Botanic Garden is located between the Santa Ynez Mountains and the Pacific Ocean. It was founded in 1926, dedicated to "the study, display, and preservation of California's native flora."

It is planted informally, with special desert, meadow, and off-shore island sections. There are lovely collections of wildflowers and fine specimens of California live oak and Douglas fir. Many rare and endangered plants are also to be found here. Five miles of nature trails offer imposing views of the mountains and ocean beyond.

Hooker's evening primroses and wildflowers in the meadow

Matilija poppies on the Porter Trail; the Santa Ynez Mountains are in the background

Succulent plants in the desert area

Manzanita with flowering yucca on the Porter Trail

Yucca with dudley and buckwheat in the meadow

Manzanita on the Porter Trail

Following: Clarkia and red-flower buckwheats in the meadow before the Santa Ynez Mountains

J. Paul Getty Museum
Malibu, California

The formal elegance of a first-century Roman villa is recaptured in the J. Paul Getty Museum and its gardens. The museum is a faithful recreation of the Villa dei Papiri, overlooking the Bay of Naples. Buried by the eruption of Vesuvius in A.D. 79, the villa was discovered in the eighteenth century by archaeologists and treasure seekers; floor plans and notes prepared at the time of the discovery made the villa's reproduction possible.

The five gardens, also based on excavations, cover twelve acres and offer a superb example of a Roman villa garden with their colonnades, statuary, pools, fountains, and carefully selected trees, shrubs, herbs, and flowers. The one thousand plantings, among them pomegranate trees and olive groves on the ramped terraces, all might have been grown in the original Roman garden.

In the Main Peristyle Garden, a long reflecting pool and bronze statues are framed by clipped shrubs and trees. The statues are modern casts of those unearthed during the eighteenth-century excavations; the originals are in the Archaeological Musuem in Naples. Adjoining the Main Garden is the Herb Garden. The smaller, enclosed East, West, and Inner Peristyle gardens feature fountains and mural paintings, patterned after the frescoes of Pompeii.

J. Paul Getty, at one time reputed to be the world's richest man, built the museum when his art collection outgrew his Malibu mansion. It includes Greek and Roman paintings, illuminated manuscripts, and European and American photography. The gardens and museum were opened to the public in 1974, two years before Getty's death.

The Main Peristyle Garden and Reflecting Pool

View of the Main Garden

Sweet peas cascade over a wall in the Herb Garden; date palms and olive trees are in the background

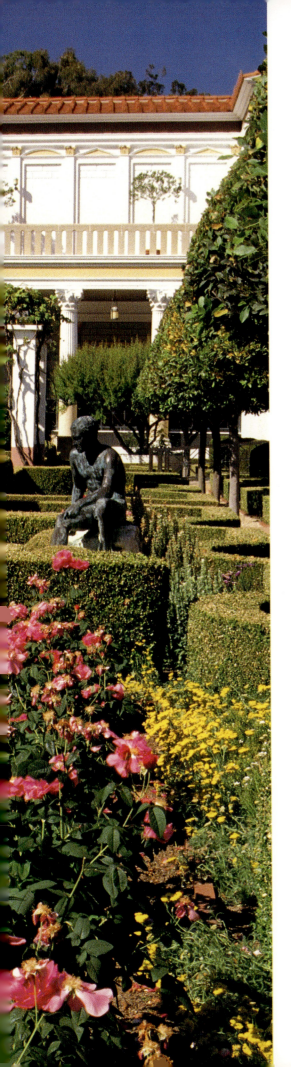

Left: Pink roses and yellow yarrow are surrounded by boxwood hedges; the museum facade is in the background

Sycamore trees in the enclosed East Garden

Boxwood hedges and red and yellow columbine in the Inner Peristyle Garden

Circular bench flanked by oleanders

Descanso Gardens
La Canada, California

This sprawling ranchland in southern California was given as part of a land grant in 1784 to a Spanish soldier from the governor of California. (California was governed by the Spaniards—and then the Mexicans—from the 1500s until the middle of the nineteenth century.)

The chaparral-covered hills and valleys were originally known as Rancho San Raphael. In 1937 E. Manchester Boddy, owner and editor of the Los Angeles Daily News, bought 165 acres of the land, re-naming it Rancho del Descanso, or Ranch of Rest.

Boddy established the gardens for his growing camellia collection, which soon became the largest in the world. Today, eighty acres of the land are open as display gardens. Among these are rose gardens, which include both an "Old Fashioned" section planted with varieties that date back thousands of years, through to the "Modern" section, with award-winning rose selections.

A stream flows peacefully through the forest of California live oaks, which shade the spectacular camellias and azaleas growing beneath. There is also a preserve of native California flora, designed to show the best uses for drought-resistant plants in erosion control.

The Japanese Tea House and Garden add a subdued element to the year-round pageantry of blossoms elsewhere in the gardens. The Hospitality House, overlooking the lovely gardens, was originally built in 1939 by Boddy as his residence; today it is an art gallery and administration building. The gardens are maintained by the Los Angeles County Department of Arboreta and Botanic Gardens.

Pacific giant delphiniums by the entrance to the Gardens

Left: A bed of Pacific giant delphiniums underplanted with dianthus

Old fashioned Newport fairy roses

A mixed border with pink Penstemon

California poppies in the Native Flora Garden

Los Angeles State and County Arboretum
Arcadia, California

Established on the site of an old Spanish mission in the foothills of the San Gabriel Mountains, the Los Angeles Arboretum is not only a magnificent horticultural showplace, but a bird sanctuary and a historic district.

The gardens were founded in 1947 on over one hundred acres at the eastern edge of the Los Angeles basin. The forty-five hundred varieties of plants are grouped in regional gardens: Australian, Asian, African, South American, and North American sections. There is also the Prehistoric and Jungle Garden and indoor gardens—greenhouses of spectacular orchids, begonias, and tropical plants.

The Lasca Lagoon, a marshland planted with papyrus and coral trees, is also a bird sanctuary, serving as a resting ground for migratory birds as well as home to year-round species. Peacocks, first introduced to the land over a century ago, still wander around the Arboretum grounds.

The historic district of the Arboretum gives one an idea of early California life. A lovely Victorian cottage built by Elias Baldwin in 1886 has recently been restored. One of the early inhabitants of the land, the fifty-eight-year-old Baldwin had the cottage built for his fourth wife, the sixteen-year-old Lillie. There is also an 1890 railroad depot, moved from nearby Sierra Madre. Both this and the cottage are State Historical Landmarks. A third building on the property dates from 1839, when the Arboretum land was part of the enormous thirteen-thousand-acre Rancho Santa Anita, owned by the anthropologist Hugo Reid. Reid married a Native American and they lived together in the adobe that still stands on the Arboretum land.

Bougainvillea in full bloom over the Lagoon; the Victorian-style cottage is in the distance

Water lilies and parrot feathers in the Aquatic Garden on top of Tallac Knoll

Meyberg Waterfall surrounded by pines, junipers, and ferns

Cattleyes surrounded by cymbidium in the Tropical Greenhouse

Pink, red, and white pansy orchids surround butterfly orchids in the Tropical Greenhouse

The Huntington
San Marino, California

In 1903 the railroad magnate Henry Edwards Huntington bought six hundred sprawling acres of ranchland in the foothills of southern California. Soon after buying the land, Huntington retired there and directed his attention to constructing his new home, augmenting his superb art and manuscript collection, and taming the chaparral and wild scrub of his vast property.

Huntington was a perfectionist. He had every one of the rooms to his new home designed and built in England and then shipped over to America; his art collection, which soon earned the reputation as the best collection of British art outside of Britain, also became one of America's most comprehensive manuscript libraries, including a fifteenth-century Gutenberg Bible, a First Folio of Shakespeare's works, and a draft of the United States Constitution. To his gardens, as well, Huntington applied these exacting standards and his passion for art and art history. His formal and botanical gardens are today, like his art works, among the finest in the Western world—both scholastically and aesthetically.

Huntington hired William Hertrich as "curator" of the grounds. Hertrich remained with the Gardens for over sixty years. In the Rose Garden are twelve hundred varieties of the flower, in historical sequence from the Middle Ages to the twentieth century. The year-round Shakespeare Garden displays only those plants that would have been grown in the dramatist's day. The Herb Garden is meticulously organized according to use: tea herbs in one section, medicinal herbs in another, those for cooking, salads, liqueurs, or perfumes are all carefully distinguished. But together the herbs create a heady olfactory experience. The Desert Garden contains the largest outdoor planting of cacti in the country. The Japanese Garden, planted with bamboo and bonsai also contains a traditional Zen Garden for quiet contemplation. The two Camellia Gardens bloom from winter through spring and among the fifteen hundred species, contain some camellias that grow to the size of trees.

Acknowledging the value of his garden and art collections, Huntington dedicated his home and land as a public institution for the advancement of learning and promotion of social welfare.

A bed of white French lace roses encircles L'Amour Captif de la Jeunesse, *an eighteenth-century French sculpture*

Left: *A weeping willow shades the Koi Pond planted with yellow irises and water lilies*

A border of irises along the rose garden

Winter plantings of yellow and purple lobelias border the lawn of the Shakespeare Garden

A mixed planting of asters

Azaleas and eighteenth-century French sculpture mark the entrance to the Camellia Garden

Left: Golden barrel cacti and other cacti species in the Desert Garden

The Desert Garden aflame with the orange-red blooms of aloe plants

Mexican golden barrel cacti and a carpet of African succulents in the Desert Garden

Straight-ribbed columnar cactus behind a bed of ice plants

Balboa Park
San Diego, California

Balboa Park is the cultural hub of San Diego; it contains five theaters, an outdoor sculpture collection, the Art Institute, a photography museum, the Natural History Museum, an aerospace museum, as well as a number of outstanding gardens.

The vast property—some twelve hundred acres—was designated a public park in 1868, but was largely neglected until the end of the century. At this time, an enterprising gardener, Kate Sessions, rented some of the land from the city and, in return, kept the canyons and mesas planted with palms, eucalyptus, and sweet gums. The park officially re-opened in 1915 as the site of the California International Exhibition, in celebration of the opening of the Panama Canal.

Scattered throughout the huge park are a rose garden, a desert garden, a lily pond, reflecting pools with aquatic plants, and a camellia-filled canyon. There are also formal English and Spanish gardens, a Spanish Village containing a cluster of artists' studios, and the Moorish Alcazar Courtyard Garden, designed after a castle in Seville. Beyond the lily pond is the Botanic Building, formerly a Santa Fe railroad station house. It is a lovely lath-roofed structure holding an impressive collection of tropical and subtropical plants and ferns.

Colorful pots of blooming annuals—pansies, impatiens, lobelias—in the Spanish Village

Left: Bougainvillea and morning glory shade baskets of petunias, alyssums, and nasturtiums

Baskets of flowering annuals in the Spanish Village

The Marston House Formal Garden

Bougainvillea in the Spanish Village

Above and left: Lily Pond and Botanical Building, built in 1915. Inside grow philodendrons, palms, impatiens, orchids, and ferns

Quail Botanical Gardens
Encinitas, California

In 1957 Ruth Baird Larabee donated her private estate and extensive plant collection to the County of San Diego. The gardens have been developed by the Quail Botanical Gardens Foundation since 1961, and now have one of the most diverse collections in the world.

The most varied bamboo collection in the country and the largest hibiscus collection on the West Coast are to be found here. There is also an outstanding display of palms and cycads—a family of ancient tropical plants related to both palms and ferns.

Among the secluded sections are the Waterfall and Palm Canyon, the Walled Garden, a subtropical fruit garden, a herb garden, a desert garden, and the lovely Old Fashioned Garden, which looks out over the ocean.

Areas are devoted to plants native to Australia, South Africa, the South Pacific, and North and Central America, but emphasis has been placed on Californian and subtropical flowering plants.

Annual flower displays in the Old Fashioned Garden

Dallas Arboretum and Botanical Garden
Dallas, Texas

The sixty-six acres comprising the Dallas Arboretum and Botanical Garden are designed to function both as a showcase and a "living laboratory" for study and research. They are divided into twenty-five acres of ornamental and research gardens and forty-one acres of woodlands and rolling meadows.

The ornamental areas are notable for their variety and color. Among them are: an octagon-shaped Bermuda grass lawn bordered by beds of seasonal flowers; trellises covered by trumpet vines; masses of azaleas, hydrangeas, and violets framed by crape myrtles and holly hedges; a redwood arbor decorated by yellow jessamine; and a magnolia allée.

The most intricately landscaped area is a two-acre ornamental garden modeled on the English perennial cottage garden. Designed to utilize both native Texas plants and other plants adaptive to the local climate, it numbers more than five hundred varieties of perennials and two hundred varieties of woody plants. The garden includes a limestone-walled pergola covered with wisteria, a dipping well, and ponds filled with water lilies and exotic fish, such as comets. Its White Garden features perennials with white blossoms or silver-gray foliage—the white color maintained throughout the year by different seasonal plants such as daffodils in spring and chrysanthemums in fall. In its Hidden Garden, concealed at first by evergreens, red oaks shade ferns and columbines that are scattered over limestone rocks. Other decorative gardens in the twenty-five acre area include the Rose Garden, with several varieties of tea roses, and the Tropical Garden, simulating a Mexican courtyard with a fountain, oleanders, hibiscus, and potted tropicals.

The education program has developed several demonstration gardens in which all plants are labeled to eliminate guesswork. The Herb Garden displays a wide range of herbs used in the kitchen. The Vegetable Garden shows how vegetables can be ornamental as well as useful. The gardens are managed by the Dallas Arboretum and Botanical Society.

The historic DeGolyer Gardens

Left: Daffodils and tulips during "Dallas Bloom," the Arboretum's spring festival

Spring-flowering primulas

Tropical water lilies in "Mimi's" Garden

Waves of purple pansies in the Arboretum's color display beds
Following: Each spring thousands of flowering bulbs blossom at the Arboretum

Above and right: Tulips and pansies in bloom along White Rock Lake

Left and above: The Margaret Elizabeth Jonsson Color Garden and Pergola
Following: The Palmer Fern Dell

Fort Worth Botanic Garden
Fort Worth, Texas

Created in 1933 during the Great Depression, this was originally a rose garden, built on a former swamp. Today, the Rose Garden is only one of a variety of gardens in the 115-acre park, which contains over 2,500 types of native and exotic plants. A striking recent addition is the seven-and-one-half-acre Japanese Garden, with its pools, waterfalls, pagoda, teahouse, and oriental plants. Embodying the traditional Japanese concept of a garden as a place for meditation, relaxation, and repose, it skilfully blends trees, shrubs, stones, and water to achieve harmony and balance. Brilliantly colored Koi dart through its pools (these fish, whose unique color and size are the result of hundreds of years of selective breeding, were at one time owned exclusively by the Japanese nobility). Its Meditation Garden is of the same design as the famed Ryoan-ji Garden in Kyoto, Japan.

Other gardens in the park include a fragrance garden for the blind and a display garden with flowering annuals and miniature roses. The Rose Garden now has more than 165 varieties of roses in peak bloom in late April and October.

A ten-thousand-square-foot conservatory houses thousands of plants native to Central and South America and the Far and Middle East, and is particularly noted for its ferns and orchids. Among its trees are various types of palm, orchid, papaya, coffee, banana, and macadamia nut. Plants along its waterfalls and ponds include such intriguing names as elephant ear, bird's nest fern, bird of paradise, shrimp, and firecracker.

At any time of year, the Botanic Garden offers a pageant of vivid color: in spring, with azaleas, roses, and flowering trees such as cherry and crab apple; in summer, crape myrtles and flowering annuals; and in fall, chrysanthemums and fall foliage.

A display bed of tulips and pansies near the Rose Garden

Following: The Japanese Garden with azaleas flowering in the foreground

Left: Azaleas and a white snowball viburnum tree

A flowering crab tree between the pagoda and torii gate

Stepping stones with a moon bridge in the distance

A kasuga lantern with red azaleas in the background

Chicago Botanic Garden
Glencoe, Illinois

Built on a former marshland in 1965, the Botanic Garden is now a series of islands, lakes, and waterways. It features fine collections of native plants and demonstration gardens.

On the main island is a rose garden and the Linnaeus Heritage Center, which demonstrates the classification of plants. The Center is named after the eighteenth-century Swedish botanist Carolus Linnaeus who originated a system of classification for plants and animals that has remained the basis of modern taxonomy.

Three islands form Sansho-en, a garden landscaped in the Japanese style. The Botanic Garden also has an educational center with ten greenhouses full of tropical and desert plants.

The Culinary Herb Garden in the Home Landscape Demonstration Garden

Early summer roses around the Rose Garden fountain

Left: *Summer color in the bulb garden*

A pathway through the Rose Garden

Perennials blooming in the Waterfall Garden
Following: Keiunto—Island of the Auspicious Cloud

Lincoln Park
CHICAGO PARK DISTRICT
Chicago, Illinois

The Chicago Park District comprises nine parks with splendid gardens and conservatories—among them are Lincoln, Garfield, and Grant parks, all named for American presidents.

Lincoln Park skirts the shores of Lake Michigan. The Main Garden has more than seven acres of formal flowerbeds, lawns, fountains, and statuary. Grandmother's Garden, begun in 1893, is the oldest in the Park District. It contains a charming collection of old-fashioned plantings.

The Lincoln Park Conservatory ranks among the finest in the world. It consists of four huge, glassed buildings and eighteen propagating houses. There are the Palm, Fernery, and Cactus houses, and the Show House—where four major horticultural shows are held each year. These enclosed gardens feature fine arrays of ever-changing floral exhibits and an impressive permanent collection of exotic trees and plants—including a year-round display of rare orchids.

The Main Garden planted with pink geraniums, white salvia, black knight cannas, and yellow coleus; Bates Fountain is in the distance

Garfield Park
CHICAGO PARK DISTRICT
Chicago, Illinois

Garfield Park's Conservatory is one of the largest and finest in the world. It has an extensive collection of unusual and exotic plants, and propagating houses in which thirty thousand plants are grown each year. Displays include the Palm House, the Aroid House (for plants of the arum family which grow in swampy tropical or subtropical habitats), the Fernery (with over one hundred kinds of ferns), the Cactus House, and the main Horticultural Hall and Show House.

In the surrounding parkland is the formal garden, where annual bedding plants are arranged in different patterns each year. A large pool contains an impressive array of water lilies.

There is also a garden for the blind. This is formed by a large, raised bed containing flowers, scented plants, and vegetables. Labels are in Braille and print.

The Fernery in Garfield Park's Conservatory, built by the landscape architect Jens Jensen

Grant Park
CHICAGO PARK DISTRICT
Chicago, Illinois

Grant Park, in the Chicago Park District, contains several gardens and the Buckingham Fountain, a lakefront landmark since 1927.

The Daniel L. Flaherty Memorial Rose Garden is a public test garden laid out in the style of Versailles. It has eight thousand hybrid tea, grandiflora, and floribunda roses arranged formally in thirty-eight beds.

The Court of Presidents, a formal annual garden, offers an excellent view of Chicago's magnificent skyline, and Saint-Gauden's statue of Abraham Lincoln.

The Court of Presidents' Garden planted with two shades of pink petunias, white globe amaranths, black knight cannas, and yellow marigolds in the distance

Tea, fairy, love, and all-American beauty roses in front of Buckingham Fountain

Longue Vue
New Orleans, Louisiana

Built in 1939 for the New Orleans cotton broker Edgar B. Stern and his wife Edith Rosenwald Stern, daughter of one of the founders of Sears-Roebuck and Company, Longue Vue is one of the last great houses of an era.

The city estate covers eight acres; the Greek-revival house is decorated largely with antiques, evoking the atmosphere of eighteenth-century interiors with wood paneling taken from an English house, Queen Ann style furniture, English creamware, Chinese export porcelain, and French block-print wallpaper. But there are also some Art Deco touches, a few elements borrowed from nineteenth-century plantation designs, and the Stern's collection of modern art.

The magnificent formal garden in the Spanish Court is the focus of the garden plan. The Court was inspired by the Generalife and other fourteenth-century gardens of the Alhambra in southern Spain. A brilliant stretch of Bermuda grass, which fades in the fall, is flanked by geometric parterres and brick planters containing sweet olive, false hollies, and other evergreens. Magnolias, pines, and crape myrtles droop over from behind the walls of the court. Water flows from a fifteenth-century marble dolpin fountain from Seville; the walks are paved with French tiles.

A series of smaller gardens of carefully arranged color schemes surround the Court. There is the Portico Garden, a formal English garden, full of the pale hues of "Summer Snow" floribunda roses, "Peace" rose standards, and "Pink Perfection" camellias. The small, intimate Pan Garden is named for the statue of Pan—the patron of shepherds—which sits atop an Italian Renaissance base. Permanent plants here include polyantha and Japanese magnolia. The long, narrow Canal Garden, inspired by Portuguese gardens, shows Longue Vue's use of container plantings. Nearby is a terraced goldfish pond, surrounded by bulbs, azaleas, and a graceful dogwood tree. The gardens were first opened to the public in 1968.

The Pan Garden filled with roses; a statue of the garden's namesake, the Greek god Pan, is at the right

105

Left: Celebrating the Three Graces, *a cast-iron Victorian fountain, stands in front of the main entrance to the house*

Top: The Pond Garden, a cool shady area with petunias and impatiens bordering the pool
Bottom: The entrance to the main house is viewed through an allée of live oaks

Following: The arching jet fountain in the Loggia area of the Spanish Court, the main formal garden

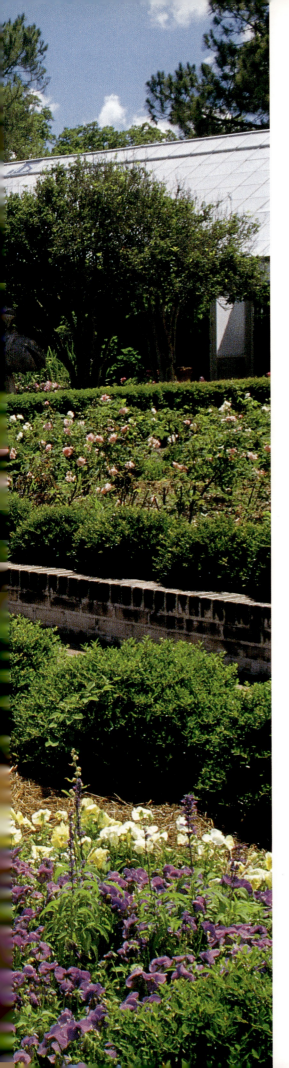

City Park
New Orleans, Louisiana

This fifteen-hundred-acre park, donated to the city of New Orleans in 1850, was at one time a plantation. Today the farmland has been converted into a series of lovely gardens, the site of the New Orleans Botanical Garden, and the New Orleans Museum of Art.

There is a huge central floral display, lovely rose gardens, and plantings of camellias, azaleas, and gardenias.

Tropical water lilies near the Conservatory

Annual Flower Pattern Bed near the Rose Garden

The fairy rose on a wattle fence in the Aromatic Garden

Homeowner's demonstration Water Garden

Vizcaya
Miami, Florida

When in 1914 the industrialist James Deering selected Miami as the site of his future winter residence, the fledgling city had a total population of ten thousand. During the next two years, under the direction of F. Burrall Hoffman, a Harvard and Ecole-des-Beaux-Arts-trained architect, one thousand workers labored day and night to build a Renaissance palazzo worthy of this prince of industry. The finished work was a splendid Italianate villa with seventy magnificent rooms (thirty-four of which are now open to the public), representing a range of styles from sixteenth-century Italy to the late eighteenth-century Neoclassicism of the Scottish architect Robert Adam.

The house took two years to build—the gardens seven. Their design was the work of Diego Suarez, a Colombian trained in Florence. His masterpiece, the ten acres of gardens at Vizcaya, reflect his Italian training. But he was not the complete purist—for certain design elements from seventeenth-century French landscape architecture are also included. In inspiration, however, the garden is completely Renaissance—that is, in its concept of the garden as an extension of the villa itself, a huge outdoor, fan-shaped room enclosed on all four sides by "walls." In Vizcaya's case the "walls" are the mangrove shoreline on one side, the subtropical hammock jungle on the other, the villa at one end, and a man-made hill (the Mount), crowned by an elegant casino, or summerhouse, at the other. Off this main room extend additional, smaller "garden rooms," the secret garden—another Italian design element—a theater garden, and a maze. Other Italianate elements include the symmetrical architectural features, clipped hedges and trees (or topiary), and shell-lined grottoes built into the sides of the Mount. Above all are the waterworks, so dear to the heart of Renaissance landscape designers: fountains, a central pond surrounding an elevated island, reflecting ponds, and a wonderful water staircase cascading down the slopes of the mountain.

Then there are the French elements—the most striking being the use of allées which lead the eye along straight vistas. Another is the parterre—low cut hedges curved into intricate patterns and admirably suited to the flat Florida terrain. True to its Italian inspiration, Vizcaya is not a flower garden but rather a stately Renaissance counterpoint of green, water, and stone. It is worth noting, however, that the traditional boxwood, cypress, or yew of Italian gardens have been replaced by ingenious adaptations to the subtropical conditions of southern Florida—parterres of jasmine and topiary of Australian pine.

A view from the gardens towards Vizcaya with an antique Italian statue of Leda and the Swan at the left

Following: The formal gardens from the south terrace of the house; white impatiens accent the lines of the clipped jasmine parterres

Left: The French-inspired Tea House on Biscayne Bay

Clipped mounds of Australian pine and white impatiens inside jasmine parterres

A view down into the Giardino Segreto, or Secret Garden

Creeping fig covers a domed gazebo; white impatiens, pink begonias, and scarlet bougainvillea are in the foreground

Fairchild Tropical Garden
Miami, Florida

In 1935 Colonel Robert Montgomery bought this site for a public botanical garden to display the collections of the famous plant explorer David Fairchild. Today, the eighty-three-acre garden is internationally known for its collection of trees, shrubs, and plants gathered from all corners of the globe. Its palm collection, the world's largest, includes more than five hundred species, many of them collected by Fairchild. Providing a fitting showcase for this remarkable collection is its beautiful setting, the result of superb landscape design by William Lyon (a pupil of Frederick Law Olmsted, celebrated designer of New York City's Central Park). Sweeping vistas, eight lakes, winding paths, and "surprise" views make this garden an aesthetic as well as educational experience for the visitor.

The unusual settings and plants are particularly noteworthy. The rain forest area simulates the humid conditions of a real rain forest by means of specially designed sprinklers. As in all tropical forests, plant life is layered: tall trees form the canopy, shorter trees the understory, and shrubs the ground flora. The sunken garden, formed in a naturally occurring sinkhole, has a fountain, many beautiful plantings, and walls bounded by tall palms. The Cycad Circle features an important display of cycads, large palm-like plants which pre-dated flowering plants by some fifty million years, and today are disappearing as their habitats are destroyed. The Rare Plant House assembles in a tropical setting rare, difficult to grow plants such as the breadfruit tree. It includes a glassed-in section for the magnificent orchid collection and a house with a lath roof, for shelter from sun and wind, which is filled with herbaceous tropicals and bromeliads (plants with brightly colored flowers and spiky leaves). The flowering plant section displays a vivid panorama of tropical and subtropical trees, shrubs, and vines that produce flowers. Red and orange flowers predominate since the eyes of nectar-eating birds, the chief pollinators in the tropics, are especially sensitive to these colors. Exotic tropical fruits grown here include the delicious-tasting sapodilla fruit, the star fruit, and the mammee apple, which is made into a liqueur in the Caribbean. An extensive program of research is conducted by the Garden staff at nearby Montgomery Foundation (named after the Garden's founder) in collaboration with scientists at other institutions.

The Liberty Hyde Bailey Palm Glade

A view of the Rare Plant House

A plant from the Agave family in the Arid Garden

Female cone of a cycad, part of the propagation program for endangered species at Fairchild

The shaving brush, a tropical flowering tree

Four Arts Garden
Palm Beach, Florida

The Four Arts Garden represents a remarkable horticultural achievement—twelve uniquely different gardens, each with its own theme, compressed into a single acre. It encompasses an amazing variety of tropical and subtropical plants. The Garden was created in 1938 by the Four Arts Society (so named for its promotion of painting, music, literature, and art) to show homeowners the kinds of gardens that could be constructed in the Palm Beach area. It shares its site with a library, art gallery, and museum. Of its gardens, four merit particular attention.

The Chinese Garden, which ranks as the Four Arts pièce de resistance, is designed to be as authentic as possible. It is completely walled except for a "moon gate" bearing an inscription that eloquently summarizes the Chinese approach to gardens with the Chinese characters meaning "health and happiness." All elements have been carefully selected and positioned according to the symbolic value attributed to them by the Chinese: the rocks, signifying mountains; the pool, representing life-sustaining water; the winding paths, warding off evil for "evil walks in a straight line;" the trees and plants, depicting human virtues, such as bamboo, which represents human hardiness and resilience. The overall emphasis is on restraint and symmetry so that the garden has an uncluttered, well-balanced look. Since, unlike the Japanese, the Chinese love color in their gardens, there are brilliantly colored flowering herbs and shrubs. Contributing to the garden's authenticity are its antique Chinese statues (the Foo dogs are from the tenth century).

In the Jungle Garden, palms encircling an irregularly shaped pool filled with fish and white water lilies create a jungle effect—an impression augmented by a variety of other tropical trees and shrubs. The Spanish Facade is dominated by a Mediterranean-style patio with a central wishing well covered in creeping fig, a bench of colorful Portuguese tiles, and two Italian cypresses in terra-cotta urns flanking its entrance. In the Fountain Garden, the emphasis is on formality. A fountain stands in an octagonal pool of multicolored water lilies, set in the middle of a lawn. The Garden is maintained by members of the Garden Club of Palm Beach, a member of the Garden Club of America.

The "moon gate" into the Chinese Garden

Left: Tenth-century stone dogs guard the entrance to the Chinese Garden

Inside the Chinese Garden

Portuguese tiles of the Spanish Facade

Callaway Gardens
Pine Mountain, Georgia

The magnificent Callaway Gardens were opened to the public in 1952, twenty years after the textile industrialist Cason J. Callaway and his wife Virginia bought twenty-five hundred acres of impoverished land in western Georgia. Determined to preserve the natural flora of the area, the Callaways embarked on a rigorous rehabilitation project. They restored forests, excavated lakes, planted gardens, and ran miles of roads and flower-filled trails through the enormous property. They also stocked the lakes for fishing, built tennis courts, golf courses, and a mile-long stretch of in-land "beach." Gradually they transformed miles of land wasted by agricultural mismanagement into one of America's finest gardens—as well as a major southern vacation resort.

The Callaways and their horticultural advisers re-introduced native plant species to the wasted land, and also experimented with more exotic, or endangered species. The most remarkable display of their careful horticultural selection and experimentation is the Azalea Trail, which features over seven hundred varieties of the spring flowering plant. Some of the varieties are indigenous to the area, but others were imported from Europe and Asia; the Callaways are also credited with rescuing the plum-leaf azalea from extinction. There are several other small gardens within the vast, wooded parkland, including a seven-acre vegetable garden, holly trails, magnolia and flowering quince, as well as a spectacular range of wildflowers. Five acres of greenhouse and a formal garden show the plant world in a tamer atmosphere.

The Gardens have indeed succeeded in fulfilling the Callaway's goal of preserving the native southeastern flora—augmenting it with that of the world.

Hanging baskets of Martha Washington geraniums at the John A. Sibley Horticultural Center

Left: Mountain Creek Lake

A spring display of Easter lilies and hanging baskets of pink hydrangeas

Easter lilies, azaleas, and grape hyacinths in the indoor/outdoor Sibley Horticultural Center

Atlanta Botanical Garden
Atlanta, Georgia

The Atlanta Botanical Garden was started in 1977 on sixty acres of land rented from the city's Piedmont Park. Today it is a lovely oasis in downtown Atlanta. Still a relatively young garden, it is continuously changing and expanding. At present, there are three main components to the Garden: the Conservatory, the Woods, and the gardens themselves.

The Fuqua Conservatory, a recent addition, was built in 1989 as a gift from a local business man, J. B. Fuqua, in honor of his wife. This houses endangered species, as well as tropical, desert, and Mediterranean plants.

The Storza Woods—fifteen acres of restored hardwood forest—is a reminder of the city's original habitat. The gardens, designed as demonstration plantings to inspire gardeners and landscape designers, are composed of rose, herb, rock, Japanese, and fragrance gardens. Elegant statuary adorns several garden ponds.

Anthurium (left) and orchids grow by the waterfall in the Tropical Rotunda of the Fuqua Conservatory

Golds and purple dianthus bloom in the spring Rock Garden

The entrance gardens beneath a sprawling paulownia tree in full bloom

A ceramic fountain is accented by aquatic plants and containers of seasonal annuals

Magnolia Plantation
Charleston, South Carolina

Listed on the National Register of Historic Places, the gardens of Magnolia Plantation rank among America's oldest and most beautiful. Held by the Drayton family continuously since 1676, the five-hundred-acre property is now owned and operated by the ninth generation descendents of the original owners. The garden encompasses fifty acres, the remainder consisting of a wildlife refuge with lakes for canoeing and nature trails.

Originally, the estate functioned as a rice plantation, with a French-style formal garden of landscaped lawns and symmetrical flowerbeds surrounding the family mansion. In the 1840s, the Reverend John Grimke-Drayton redesigned it along more informal lines, fostering its natural vegetation, and using exotics for color and adornment. He introduced and planted numerous azaleas and camellias. During the Civil War the Plantation was torched by Sherman's troops, marking the end of its rice cultivation. However, the garden was salvaged by Grimke-Drayton, and gradually restored. Slowly, its fame began to spread. It was opened to the public by popular demand in the late 1860s. By 1900, Baedecker's travel guide was recommending Magnolia Gardens, along with Niagara Falls and the Grand Canyon, as one of the three major attractions in America.

Today, the great avenue of magnolias that gave the garden its name is gone but handsome specimens are scattered throughout the grounds, which also include live oaks draped with Spanish moss, cypress trees and redwoods. In spring, climbers like mauve wisteria, yellow banksia rose, and white Cherokee rose brighten the branches of the trees, and masses of flowering fruit trees—cherry and apple together with jonquils and violets—display their colors.

The Plantation's other features include a camellia maze modeled after the celebrated maze in Hampton Court, England, created in the sixteenth century for Henry VIII; an eighteenth-century-style herb garden; a small garden of Biblical plants; and a garden of native plants.

Magnolia Plantation House viewed from the Ashley River

Above: "Long Bridge" spanning a cypress lake

Left: Stately cypress trees and a vivid band of azaleas are reflected in the black-water lake, one of the Gardens many secluded gazebos is in the background

Left: Cypress Pond bordered with vari-colored azaleas

The Vineyard Boy, *an Italian garden statue, within a mass of azaleas*

"Flower Dale," the original 1680s garden designed in the formal Italian style

A gazebo hidden in a sunny glade of azaleas

Middleton Place
Charleston, South Carolina

Middleton Place is the oldest landscaped garden in the United States. Begun in 1741 by Henry Middleton, a landowner, planter, and one of the most influential political figures of his time, the sixty-five-acre garden lies on an estate of six thousand acres. It took one hundred slaves ten years to complete. Since its settlement it has been held by the same family.

Unlike any other in the country at that time, the garden was landscaped in the formal symmetrical and precise style developed by the famed French seventeenth-century landscape architect André le Nôtre, who laid out Louis XIV's gardens at Versailles. Le Nôtre's concept of a central, uninterrupted vista is embodied in the garden's central axis. It runs straight through the ruins of the main house, down a succession of terraces, and between the Butterfly Lakes (twin lakes shaped like a butterfly's open wings) to the river until it disappears in the distant marsh. The garden's formal areas include: a rectangular pool inhabited by swans; an octagonal sunken garden; a wheel-shaped sundial garden; a bamboo grove; a "secret" garden designed for intimate family gatherings; and a camellia garden (America's first camellias were planted here in the late eighteenth century by a visiting French botanist).

A well-known landmark is the Middleton Oak, said to be more than a thousand years old; it has a circumference of thirty feet, a limb spread of forty-five feet, and is eighty-five-feet tall.

Middleton Place has survived a violent history. Plundered during the Revolution, burnt at the end of the Civil War (its owner at the time, William Middleton, supported the Confederate cause), and devastated by the Great Earthquake of 1886, it lay neglected until its restoration in 1916. A vivid reminder of its troubled past is the marble wood nymph who sits above the Azalea Pond. Prior to the arrival of the Union troops, William Middleton buried her in the garden. She is now Middleton's logo.

Azalea Hillside near the Rice Mill Pond

Left: Rice Mill Pond Bridge

The Wood Nymph *(c. 1810), once one of many statues in the gardens before the Civil War*

The Sundial and Rose Garden lie beyond a bush of azaleas

The Middleton Oak—over a thousand years old—marked an Indian trail before the English settled Carolina

Monticello
Charlottesville, Virginia

Thomas Jefferson began construction of Monticello in 1769—when he was only twenty-six years old—on a small mountain (or monti-cello, *in Italian) overlooking Virginia's rolling farmland and the Blue Ridge Mountains. He centered his house on a level plot of land, around which he laid out a series of oval "Roundabouts," woods, gardens, and orchards. The grounds became a kind of living laboratory for the study of botany, agriculture, and landscape architecture.*

A governor, foreign minister, secretary of state, vice-president, and ultimately the third president of the United States, Jefferson was also a progressive farmer, botanist, and an architect who designed his home, its furnishings, and the layout of his land. His plans for the gardens of Monticello were in the English park style—an ironic choice from the author of the Declaration of Independence. However, as Jefferson wrote, the gardening in that country "surpasses all the earth." He designed a naturalistic landscape softened by the winding paths with flower borders, a Grove of ornamental trees, a vegetable garden, and fish pond.

Jefferson was an avid believer in horticultural experimentation. He tested over two hundred and fifty varieties of vegetables and herbs, including nearly twenty varieties of the English pea, his favorite vegetable. Many of these varieties are still grown today in his thousand-foot vegetable garden.

Few early American gardens are as well documented as those at Monticello. Jefferson's detailed records, kept in his Garden Book, along with recent archaeological discoveries, have made possible an accurate recreation of his gardening scheme.

Poppies along the Roundabout; the west facade of Monticello is in the background

Left: Larkspur and Canterbury bells frame the view of Monticello's west facade

Sweet William (red) and larkspur (purple) on the Roundabout Flower Walk

The one-thousand-foot-long Vegetable Garden; Carolina lima beans are trained on poles

Larkspur growing among sea kale in the Vegetable Garden

Dumbarton Oaks
Washington, D.C.

Dumbarton Oaks has been called "one of the last great private gardens to be created in this century." Bought by Mr. and Mrs. Robert Woods Bliss in 1920, the sixteen-acre garden comprises a series of terraces built on a hill behind an eighteenth-century Georgian-style mansion. At the time of its purchase, its grounds were neglected and crowded with numerous barnyards and cowpaths. Its transformation was made possible by the combined creative efforts of Mrs. Bliss and noted landscape architect Beatrice Farrand. For twenty-five years the two worked together to create the garden, making mock-ups of each item, no matter how small, and putting them in place before making any final decisions.

The overall plan incorporates three principles. First, there is progressive informality in the designs, materials, and plantings as the gardens descend the slope. Second, plants are selected for beauty and interest in the winter as well as the spring and autumn. Third, the gardens represent an extension of the house, with enclosed areas or "rooms" for family living and entertaining. For example, the Star Garden, so called because of its astrological motifs and relief of Aquarius, is designed for family dining. A miniature theater, modeled after one near Rome, seats fifty people. Other courtyard-terrace areas include the swimming pool, the Pebble Garden (formerly the tennis court) where a pebble mosaic of a wheat sheaf (part of the Bliss family coat-of-arms) glimmers under a thin layer of water from a fountain; the Rose Garden, the Blisses' favorite part of the garden, where nearly one thousand roses are planted; and the Ellipse, comprising a circular fountain set in a lawn and ringed by walks and clipped trees.

Dumbarton Oaks was given by the Blisses to Harvard University in 1940, and the gardens were opened to the public shortly afterwards.

The Fountain Terrace, a formal Italian-style garden
Following: The Pebble Garden

Top: *A view of the Arbor Terrace from the wisteria arbor*

Bottom: *The Rose Garden—pink tiffany and red scarlet knight roses*

Top: The Arbor Terrace with blue plumbagos, red geraniums, and yellow lantanas; wisteria grows in the background

Bottom: The Arbor from the Fountain Terrace; white physostegias, yellow pansies, and red and yellow gaillardias bloom in the foreground

Different views of a herbaceous border with yellow pansies, red dahlias, pink Lythrum, *pink hollyhocks, red monardas, and yellow coreopsis; the tool shed can be seen in the distance*

Winterthur
Winterthur, Delaware

Winterthur is one of the finest and loveliest examples in this country of the English "naturalistic" style of landscape gardening. The estate had been in the possession of the du Pont family since 1839 when Eveline Gabrielle du Pont de Nemours and her husband James A. Biderman bought the property and named it after his hometown in Switzerland. However, the gardens as they now stand are the creation and crowning achievement of Henry Frances du Pont who inherited the 960-acre estate in 1927 and continued to develop and enhance its 200 acres of gardens right up until his death in 1969.

A passionate and meticulous landscape gardener, du Pont was not only gifted with an artist's eye but was also a learned and knowledgeable botanist—a true connoisseur of plants. Taking as his starting point the rolling hills and woods of the Delaware countryside, du Pont proceeded to enhance and add to his gardens with exotic and rare plants—many from the Far East. The result looks entirely natural—but is, in fact, planned right down to every last detail, including the exact placing of azalea bushes for the most aesthetically pleasing color scheme. Wildflowers grow in profusion—but the bluebells are from Spain, the buttercups from Siberia, the anemones from Italy, and the primulas from the Himalayas.

Among the glories of Winterthur are the Azalea Woods made more glorious by du Pont with the introduction of famous Dexter rhododendrons; the Pinetum with its more than sixty-three species of conifers, many exceedingly rare; the March Bank, at its most brilliant in the spring; the Chandler Woods, a natural Eastern woodland that is home to the three-hundred-year-old William Penn tree; and the Quarry Garden, an enchanted idyll created out of an abandoned quarry and featuring amidst its gently flowing streams Himalayan primulas, wild marsh marigolds and other native and exotic bog and rock plants. There are only two formal gardens—one is the Sundial Garden and the other the garden adjoining the house itself.

Rhododendrons and daffodils in the Pinetum

Left: Sargent cherry trees along Garden Lane

Daffodils growing along Pavilion Drive

The Winterhazel area with blue scilla on the ground

Forsythia on the edge of the Azalea Woods

Left: The Sundial Garden with magnolias and cherry trees in bloom

The armillary sundial in the Sundial Garden with flowering quince in the foreground

View of the "Lavender Queen" azalea growing along the March Bank

Nemours
Wilmington, Delaware

At the opposite end of the landscape design spectrum from Winterthur—the quintessential English-style "naturalistic" garden—is nearby Nemours, also a du Pont creation but one that embraces a totally different tradition—that of the highly stylized French formal garden. The chateau, seventeenth century and French in inspiration, was completed by 1910, the gardens by 1932. Alfred I. du Pont, builder of the chateau, sent his son Alfred Victor to France to study garden design. The young Alfred succumbed completely to the continental tastes and the resulting French influence at Nemours is total. A mini-Versailles was created in the Delaware countryside, including a garden in the grand seventeenth-century manner, designed to impress, dazzle, and awe. The gardens at Versailles were designed by André le Nôtre, garden architect to Louis XIV. Those at Nemours are a twentieth-century, scaled-down replica, faithful to all but one le Nôtre principle: instead of a main axis extending into a seemingly limitless vista, the vista at Nemours is blocked by a huge colonnade, behind which is a second garden leading to a second vista—the Temple of Love with, as its focal point, a statue of Diana by the eighteenth-century sculptor Antoine Houdon.

However, all the other major elements of le Nôtre's design at Versailles may be found replicated at Nemours—right down to the wooden tubs for the terrace trees which are exact copies of those used at Versailles to hold three thousand royal orange trees. There are the tree-lined allées, the formal low-cut parterres, abundant use of statuary and fountain displays—the one in the Reflecting Pool alone has 157 jets. True to the French tradition, design and architecture at Nemours are paramount; the plants themselves secondary.

When the gardens were completed in 1932, they were opened to the public for one day only—at a cost of $1 per visitor. With this one notable exception, public interest was very distinctly discouraged by Alfred du Pont, who surrounded his three-hundred-acre estate with a high wall topped with broken glass to keep the rabble (including other du Ponts) at bay.

The Nemours mansion

Left: Weeping fig trees frame this view of the mansion across the Maze Garden

A bed of salvia and coleus lead to the Reflecting Pool

A French parterre garden planted with English boxwood, pink begonias, vinca, and blue ageratum

Left: The Grape Arbor

Hedges of Canadian hemlock and Helleri holly in the Maze Garden

Carrara marble statuary in the Sunken Garden

The Temple of Love viewed from the fleurs-de-lis parterre filled with begonias

Longwood Gardens
Kennett Square, Pennsylvania

In 1700 a Quaker family named Peirce purchased two hundred acres of land from William Penn for their farm. The family and its descendents farmed the land and planted ornamental trees throughout it, creating one of America's first tree parks. Early in this century, the land was threatened by lumbering interests until Pierre S. du Pont, who later became chairman of General Motors and the du Pont Company, purchased the entire property, preserving the arboretum and beginning construction of the spectacular horticultural conservatories. The gardens were first opened to the public in 1921 and are considered today among the country's finest gardens.

The park has now grown to over one thousand acres; more than three hundred of which are gardens open to the public. The gardens encompass a broad range of design traditions, but in overall scope are best compared to the Renaissance pleasure gardens of Italy and France.

The Renaissance passion for spectacular water displays was well matched by that of Pierre S. du Pont. Originally trained as an engineer, he delighted in carrying off elaborate hydraulic feats. There is an open-air theater, modeled after that at Villa Gori near Siena, which was designed with hundreds of hidden fountains. The Italian Water Garden, based on a garden at Villa Gamberaia outside of Florence, contains a water staircase and water parterres. Then there is the Fountain Garden, du Pont's great joy, inspired by le Nôtre's creations at Versailles.

For the meadows and flower gardens, however, du Pont drew on English inspiration. He left untouched fields of wildflowers and natural woodlands, as expounded by Capability Brown's "Park style" of landscaping; and the formal flowerbeds of riotous color are strictly in keeping with Victorian tastes. The conservatories are among Longwood's stellar horticultural achievements. Filled with spectacular floral displays, they cover several acres and include fine collections of orchids, ferns, roses, palms, and desert plants. There is also an enormous rock garden, informal gardens of bulbs, annuals, and perennials, and the lovely Rose Arbor, covered through the summer with climbing roses.

A fountain in the East Conservatory bordered with brilliant geraniums

Left: Pink zinnias, red cockscomb, and chartreuse coleus along the Flower Garden Walk

Yellow lantanas, orange-red zinnias, cannas (yellow), and red salvia

Petunias, Siberian irises, and blue salvia

Mixed cockscomb, blue salvia, and pink begonias

The Italian Water Garden modeled after that at Villa Gamberaia, near Florence

One of Longwood's "Love Temples" overlooking a large lake

Following: An allée of caryopteris with yellow sternbergia leads to one of Longwood's three "Love Temples"

Left: A topiary garden above one of Longwood's "Love Temples"

The Rose Arbor with American pillar roses

Purple physostegia and asters surrounding silver artemisia; goldenrod adds a touch of yellow

An annuals display in the Idea Garden including red cockscomb and blue salvia

The Cloisters
New York, New York

With its medieval campanile breaking anachronistically through the trees of Fort Tryon Park, The Cloisters of The Metropolitan Museum of Art adds an eerily beautiful silhouette to the Manhattan skyscape. Positioned on one of the islands highest points, The Cloisters was completed in 1938, an assemblage of five medieval French monasteries, a twelfth-century chapter house from a ruined abbey in Gascony, France, a Romanesque chapel, and a twelfth-century Spanish apse.

There are three main gardens at The Cloisters—one beneath the covered arcades of the Cuxa Cloister, a herb garden in the Bonnefont Cloister, and the Trie Cloister garden. A fourth small indoor garden in the Saint-Guilhem Cloister houses pots of grape hyacinth, crocus, and narcissus in the spring.

The Cuxa Courtyard Garden, planted in quadrants around a fountain, is primarily a fragrant garden filled with aromatic plants such as jasmine, sage, and rosemary. The plantings of the Trie Cloister are based on those found in The Cloisters' Unicorn Tapestries—a splendid series of tapestries from the sixteenth century depicting the capture of the fantastical medieval creation, the unicorn. Surrounding the main subject of each tapestry is a carpet of vegetation—one of the most comprehensive sources of information on medieval botany. The plants that grow in the garden can be seen, in some cases embellished with artistic license, in the tapestries, including many species not ordinarily found in America. Among the garden's plantings are pomegranate and hazelnut trees, violets, the Madonna Lily, and wild strawberry. In the Bonnefont Cloister is a herb garden. Much of the information for these plantings came from a ninth-century botanical list compiled by Emperor Charlemagne, as a guide to the appropriate plants to grow in royal gardens of the Holy Roman Empire. Many of the plants included here—motherwort, lovage, borage, sorrel—would have typically been grown in medieval monasteries for medicinal purposes, seasoning, perfumes, or dyes.

The gardens of The Cloisters are maintained by the institution's horticultural staff.

Garden of the Cuxa Cloister with a fragrant flower border; a pear tree is in the background

Left: The Bonnefont Cloister herb garden with quince trees and a pot of miniature roses

The Cuxa Cloister garden

A Sargent crab apple behind the fountain

The Trie Cloister garden

Brooklyn Botanic Garden
Brooklyn, New York

In 1910, thanks to the efforts of a group of dedicated citizens, a botanical garden was established on a rock-strewn piece of city wasteland in the heart of Brooklyn. Today, the Brooklyn Botanic Garden is internationally known. Its fifty-two acres house more than twelve thousand plants, all labeled with their common and scientific names and country of origin, with almost every country represented.

Best known of the numerous gardens is the Japanese hill-and-pond garden. Designed in 1915 by landscape architect Takeo Shiota, it reflects the Japanese concept of the garden as a place for contemplation, a "mirror of nature." Essentially, it is a miniaturized landscape created by blending dwarfed and pruned trees and shrubs, carefully placed rocks, a small artificial "lake," and a waterfall. Unlike most Western gardens, flowering plants are used sparingly; this is virtually an evergreen garden.

Another Japanese garden is a replica of the five-hundred-year-old garden adjacent to the Ryoan-ji Buddhist Temple in Kyoto. To western eyes this garden may appear, initially at least, very strange. It features a rock arrangement on a flat surface covered with gravel meticulously raked in rippling designs. There is no hint of green except for the moss on the rocks.

A vivid contrast is provided by the various western gardens, such as a formal rose garden and the Osborne Memorial Garden with its geometric layout, dominant fountain, obelisk, banks of azaleas, and pergolas.

Other gardens include the Shakespeare Garden, containing plants mentioned in Shakespeare's plays; a herb garden resembling an Elizabethan knot garden; and a fragrance garden.

In addition to its gardens, Brooklyn Botanic offers striking displays and collections. The flowering cherry display in its Cherry Esplanade in early May is second only to that in Washington, D.C. The Magnolia Plaza is alive with blossoms in late April and May, displaying specimens from the Orient and southern United States. The bonsai (dwarf tree) collection in the Conservatory is one of America's best.

The Japanese Hill-and-Pond Garden in fall splendor

Left: The Cranford Rose Garden

The Shakespeare Garden

Water lily pools

Left: Kwanzan flowering cherry trees in the Cherry Esplanade

The Herb Garden

Here and below: Annuals along the Water Lily Pools

New York Botanical Garden
Bronx, New York

The New York Botanical Garden is one of the country's oldest—and among the world's largest—botanical collections. It was founded in 1891 by a Columbia University botanist, Nathaniel Lord Britton, who felt that New York should have a garden to rival London's Kew Gardens.

Many prominent New Yorkers rose to the challenge, including Cornelius Vanderbilt and Andrew Carnegie, both of whom served on the Garden's board of managers. Once sufficient funding had been collected, the city turned over 250 acres of land in the northern Bronx for a garden that would serve both recreational and research purposes.

The Conservatory, built in 1902 after London's Crystal Palace of 1851, has been recently restored and is today the crowning achievement of the garden's founders. The Enid A. Haupt Conservatory is made up of eleven glass pavilions and a central glass dome that soars nintey-feet high. It contains a Palm Court in the central dome, orangeries, a medieval herb garden, tropical and subtropical pavilions with exotic plants from around the world, a Fern Jungle, deserts, and a teaching center. Outside, in the courtyard, the glorious domed structure is reflected in pools of sacred lotus, papyrus, and water lilies.

The Rock Garden, planted among Ice Age glaciers, contains plants that have adapted to mountainous regions and other harsh climates, from the Rockies to the Himalayas. Despite the extreme temperatures of these terrains, one can find the most delicate and persistent of blossoms.

Nearby is the Native Plant Garden, a collection of vegetation from North-East America. Numerous other gardens are scattered throughout, there is the Rose Garden, a herb garden, a hemlock forest, as well as the Azalea Way and Rhododendron Valley. The Bronx Zoo is just across the road.

The Conservatory dome from the Bechtel Rose Garden

Above: Tropical Aquatic Pool inside the Conservatory; an Allamanda *vine is suspended from the glass roof; cycads are in the background*

Right: A clematis vine in flower

Left: *The Detour Walk planted with annuals, including canna lilies and cleomes*

Gladiolas and hostas

Irises bordering the Rock Garden Pond

The Detour Walk in spring

Wave Hill
Bronx, New York

Early this century the conservationist/banker George Walbridge Perkins bought three adjacent Hudson River estates in a section of the Bronx called Riverdale. One of them was Wave Hill, a lovely stretch of land overlooking New Jersey's Palisades. The main house on the property was begun in 1844 and was used as a residence for famous visiting artists and political figures—Mark Twain, Theodore Roosevelt, and William Makepeace Thackeray all lived there at various stages, as well as Arturo Toscanini and the British ambassador to the United Nations. In 1960 the Perkins family gave Wave Hill to the city; the three estates are today a campus of the Riverdale Country School, the Institute of Marine and Atmospheric Sciences at City College, and the Wave Hill Center for Environmental Studies.

Wave Hill covers twenty-eight acres of gardens and woodlands. There is an English-style wild garden, rose, herb, and aquatic gardens, in addition to greenhouse collections of cacti, Alpine plants, orchids, and succulents. The Center uses its spectacular setting to conduct programs in horticulture, landscape design, and forest restoration and preservation. It also provides an ideal forum for the arts, hosting site-specific sculpture, painting, or photography projects and performances that incorporate the gardens and landscapes into their settings.

Asters and amaranthus in peak fall bloom

Crimson brocade asters and "alma Potschke" are backed by brilliant dahlias and burgundy amaranthus

Hydrangeas, Japanese anemones, and spider flowers

The Wave Hill Flower Garden

The Palisades of New Jersey tower above the Hudson River and form an everpresent horizon line to the gardens

Old Westbury Gardens
Old Westbury, New York

At the beginning of this century, American industrialist John Phipps recreated a nineteenth-century English country estate on Long Island. Today, the hundred-acre estate, Old Westbury, its Georgian mansion set in an expanse of lawns, broad tree-lined avenues, reflecting pools, and distant vistas, ranks as one of the outstanding display gardens in the United States. Both the house and garden were designed by the same architect, resulting in an overall consistency in plan and execution.

The estate is distinguished by the scope and variety of its garden areas or "rooms," ranging from the formal to the practical. In the Boxwood Garden giant boxwood, already one hundred years old when transported from Virginia, line the lily pool. The Cottage Garden features a little girl's thatched cottage surrounded by a miniature garden and pink and white flowering shrubs, dogwood, hawthorn, and azaleas, as well as a rose-covered sandbox. In the Walled Garden more than two acres of flowers provide an unbroken succession of constantly changing color from early May through October. Several small demonstration gardens have been created to provide visitors with ideas and designs they can incorporate into their own gardens. Among these are a rose test garden, a herb garden, and a Japanese-style garden.

Old Westbury represents one of the few remaining examples of extensive herbaceous borders in this country. It is listed in Great Gardens of the Western World.

The Great South Lawn

Left: The Walled Garden in early summer

Chrysanthemums in the Walled Garden

Wisteria climbing the walls of the South Terrace

The Thatched Cottage and Garden

Left: The East Gate leading into the Walled Garden

Old fashioned climbing roses cover the Rose Garden trellis

The Reflecting Pool in the Boxwood Garden
Following: The Temple of Love on the banks of the East Lake

Isabella Stewart Gardner Museum
Boston, Massachusetts

The museum is the creation of Isabella Stewart Gardner (1860-1924). Her main interest was the art and architecture of Italy, and she designed her home in the style of a Venetian palazzo. The building incorporates columns, archways, and fountains from Italy. It is filled with around two thousand **objets d'art** from her personal collection. The museum was opened to the public in 1903.

Fenway Court, the glass-covered courtyard, is a highly formal garden of classical statuary, evergreens, a fountain, and a changing collection of potted flowers, set against a background of vaulted Renaissance arches. When in season, orange nasturtiums flow down the courtyard's four stories into the garden below.

The seasonal displays are a special attraction: lilies and cineraria at Easter, azaleas and jasmine in the spring, chrysanthemums and begonias in the fall, and poinsettias and cyclamen at Christmas.

The museum also features two outdoor, walled gardens. The Monk's Garden is a woodland rock garden with curved paths and Japanese ornaments. Evergreen shrubs predominate. The ground cover is English Ivy, interspersed with wildflowers. In 1977 a new formal garden was created. It has straight walks, grassy lawns, and a short avenue of Katsura trees leading to a statue of Diana, goddess of the hunt. Terra-cotta urns planted with geraniums and petunias give color to this otherwise green-and-white garden.

The courtyard garden with pots of hydrangeas

Following: The northeast corner of the courtyard

Acknowledgments

Among the many people across the country who have helped with this book over the past few years, I would like to thank in particular the gardeners, garden directors, and public relations officers who have so painstakingly preserved the gardens, kept them open to the public, and allowed me to photograph them. I would also like to thank my editor at Rizzoli, Sarah Burns, for her help in assembling this book.

M.A.

Public Garden Source List

ALABAMA

Birmingham Botanical Gardens
2612 Lane Park Road
Birmingham   35223
205-879-1576

Mobile Botanical Gardens
Museum Drive, Municipal Park
Mobile   36608
205-342-0555

Bellingrath Gardens
Route 59
(Route 1 Box 60)
Theodore   36582
205-973-2365

ALASKA

Governor's Mansion
9th Street and Calhoun Avenue
Juneau   99801
907-586-2201

ARIZONA

Desert Botanical Garden
Papago Park
5800 East Van Buren St.
6400 East McDowell Rd.
Phoenix   85008
602-941-1217

Mormon Temple Gardens
525 E. Main St.
Mesa   85203
602-964-7164

Boyce Thompson Southwestern Arboretum
Route 60
(Box AB)
Superior   85273
602-689-2811

ARKANSAS

Arkansas Territorial Restoration
Territorial Square
214 East Third Street
Little Rock   72201
501-324-9351

CALIFORNIA

Strybing Arboretum and Botanical Gardens
Japanese Tea Garden
9th Avenue Lincoln Way
San Francisco   94122
415-558-3622

Filoli
Canada Road
Woodside   94062
415-364-2880

Berkeley Botanical Garden
University of California
Berkeley   94720
415-642-3343

Hearst Castle
Hearst San Simeon State Historical Monument
750 Hearst Castle Road
San Simeon   93452
800-444-7275

Santa Barbara Botanic Garden
1212 Mission Canyon Road
Santa Barbara   93105
805-682-4726

Lotusland
695 Ashley Road
Montecito   93108
805-969-3767

J. Paul Getty Museum
17985 Pacific Coast Highway
Malibu   90265
213-459-2306

Virginia Robinson Gardens
1008 Elden Way
Beverly Hills   90210
213-276-5367

Descanso Gardens
1418 Descanso Drive
La Canada   91011
213-790-5571

The Huntington
1151 Oxford Road
San Marino   91108
818-405-2100

Los Angeles State and County Arboretum
301 North Baldwin Avenue
Arcadia   91007
213-446-8251

Quail Botanical Gardens
230 Quail Gardens Drive
Encinitas   92924
619-436-3036

Balboa Park
Laurel Street and 6th Avenue
San Diego   92112
619-239-0512

COLORADO

Denver Botanic Gardens
909 York Street
Denver   80206
303-575-2547

CONNECTICUT

White Flower Farm
Route 63 South
Litchfield   06759
203-567-8789

Bartlett Arboretum
151 Brookdale Road
Stamford   06903
203-322-6971

DELAWARE

Winterthur
Route 52
Winterthur   19735
302-654-1548

Nemours
Rockland Road off Route 141
(P.O. Box 109)
Wilmington   19899
302-651-6912

Hagley Museum
Route 100 at Route 141
(P.O. Box 3630)
Wilmington   19807
302-658-2400

DISTRICT OF COLUMBIA

Dumbarton Oaks
1703 32nd Street N.W.
Washington, D.C.   20007
202-338-8278

White House Gardens
1600 Pennsylvania Avenue
Washington, D.C.   20500
202-426-6700

U.S. National Arboretum
24th and R Streets N.E.
Washington, D.C.   20002
202-472-9279

FLORIDA

Florida Cypress Gardens
Route 540
Winterhaven   33880
813-324-2111

Four Arts Garden
Four Arts Plaza
Palm Beach   33480
305-655-2766

Vizcaya
3251 South Miami Avenue
Miami   33129
305-579-2708

Fairchild Tropical Garden
10901 Old Cutler Road
Miami   33156
305-667-1651

GEORGIA

Atlanta Botanical Garden
Piedmont Park at South Prado
(P.O. Box 77246)
Atlanta   30357
404-876-5858

State Botanical Garden of Georgia
2450 South Milledge Avenue
Athens   30605
404-542-1244

Callaway Gardens
Route 27 South
Pine Mountain   31822
404-663-2281

HAWAII

Waimea Arboretum and Botanical Garden
Waimea Falls Park
59-864 Kamehameha Highway
Haleiwa, Oahu   96712
808-638-8511

Foster Botanical Gardens
50 North Vineyard Boulevard
Honolulu   96817
808-522-7060

Harold L. Lyon Arboretum
3860 Manoa Road
Honolulu   96822
808-988-3177

Olu Pua Botanical Garden and Plantation
Route 50 West
(P.O. Box 518)
Kalaheo, Kauai 96741
808-332-8182

IDAHO

Charles Huston Shattuck Arboretum
College of Forestry
University of Idaho
Central Campus
(205 C.E.B.)
Moscow   83843
208-885-6250

ILLINOIS

Lincoln Park
Stockton Drive and Fullerton Parkway
Chicago   60614
312-294-4770

Garfield Park
300 North Central Park Boulevard
Chicago   60624
312-533-1281

Grant Park
700 South Columbus Drive
Balbo and Columbus Drive
Chicago   60605
312-294-2286

Chicago Botanic Garden
Lake Cook Road
(P.O. Box 400)
Glencoe   60022
708-835-5440

INDIANA

Christie Woods, Ball State University
Riverside and University Avenues
Muncie   47306
317-285-5341

Garfield Park Conservatory and Sunken Gardens
2450 Shelby Street
Indianapolis   46203
317-784-3044

IOWA

Arie den Boer Arboretum
Water Works Park
408 Fleur Drive
Des Moines   50321
515-283-8791

Des Moines Botanical Center
909 East River Drive
Des Moines   50316
515-283-4148

KANSAS

Bartlett Arboretum
Route 55
(P.O. Box 39)
Belle Plaine   67013
316-488-3451

Gage Park
4320 West 10th Street
Topeka   66604
913-232-1484

KENTUCKY

Bernheim Forest Arboretum
Route 245
Clermont   40110
502-543-2451

Lexington Cemetery
883 West Main Street
Lexington   40508
606-255-5522

LOUISIANA

Hodges Gardens
Route 171
(P.O. Box 900)
Many   71449
318-586-3523

Longue Vue
7 Bamboo Road
New Orleans   70124
504-488-5488

City Park
1 Dreyfus Avenue
New Orleans   70124
504-483-9386

MAINE

Asticou Azalea Garden
Asticou Way
Northeast Harbor   04662
207-276-5456

Bath Marine Museum and Garden
963 Washington Street
Bath   04530
207-443-1316

MARYLAND

Ladew Topiary Gardens
3535 Jarrettsville Pike
Monkton   21111
301-557-9466

London Town Publik House and Gardens
839 London Town Road
Edgewater   21037
301-956-4900

Brookside Gardens
1500 Glenallen Avenue
Wheaton   20902
301-949-8230

MASSACHUSETTS

Arnold Arboretum
Arborway
Jamaica Plains   02130
617-524-1718

Isabella Stewart Gardner Museum
2 Palace Road
Boston   02115
617-566-1401

Garden in the Woods
New England Wild Flower Society
Hemenway Road
Framingham   01701
617-877-6574

Heritage Plantation of Sandwich
Grove Street
Sandwich   02563
617-888-3300

MICHIGAN

W. J. Beal Botanical Garden
Michigan State University
East Lansing   48823
517-355-0348

Matthaei Botanical Gardens
University of Michigan
1800 Dixboro Road
Ann Arbor   48105
313-764-1168

Anna Scripps Whitcomb Conservatory
Belle Isle Park
Detroit   48207
313-224-1097

MINNESOTA

Minnesota Landscape Arboretum
University of Minnesota
3675 Arboretum Drive
Chaska   55317
612-443-2460

Como Park Conservatory
Midway Park
Kaufman Drive
St. Paul   55103
612-489-1740

MISSISSIPPI

Wister Henry Garden
Route 7
(P.O. Box 237)
Belzoni   39038
601-247-3025

Mynelle Gardens
4736 Clinton Boulevard
Jackson   39209
601-960-1894

MISSOURI

Missouri Botanical Gardens
2101 Tower Grove Avenue
St. Louis   63110
314-577-5100

Jewel Box
5600 Clayton Avenue
St. Louis   63110
314-535-1503

MONTANA

Memorial Rose Garden
700 Brook Street
Missoula   59801
406-721-7275

NEBRASKA

General Crook House
30th and Fort Streets
(P.O. Box 11398)
Omaha   68111
402-455-9990

Arbor Lodge State Historical Park and Arboretum
Nebraska Game and Parks Commission
Off Routes 73-75 and 2
Nebraska City   68410
402-873-3221

NEVADA

Botanical Garden
Ethel M. Chocolate Factory
2 Cactus Garden Drive
Henderson   89014
702-458-8864

NEW HAMPSHIRE

Fuller Gardens
10 Willow Avenue
North Hampton   03862
603-964-5414

Moffatt-Ladd House
154 Market Street
Portsmouth   03801
603-436-8221

NEW JERSEY

Frelinghuysen Arboretum
53 East Hanover Avenue
Morristown   07960
201-829-0474

Duke Gardens Foundation
Route 206
(P.O. Box 2030)
Somerville   08876
201-722-3700

Rutgers Recreation and Display Gardens
Cook College
Route 1 at Ryders Lane
(P.O. Box 231)
New Brunswick   08903
908-932-9325

NEW MEXICO

Living Desert State Park
Route 285
(P.O. Box 100)
Carlsbad   88220
505-887-5516

NEW YORK

New York Botanical Garden
Bronx Park
Southern Boulevard
Bronx   10458
212-220-8700

Wave Hill
675 West 252nd Street
Bronx   10471
212-549-2055

The Cloisters
Metropolitan Museum of Art
Fort Tryon Park
New York   10040
212-923-3700

Brooklyn Botanic Garden
1000 Washington Avenue
Brooklyn   11225
718-622-4433

Old Westbury Gardens
71 Old Westbury Road
Old Westbury   11568
516-333-0048

Planting Fields Arboretum
Planting Fields Road
Oyster Bay   11771
516-922-9201

NORTH CAROLINA

Sarah P. Duke Gardens
Duke University
West Campus
Durham   22706
919-684-3698

North Carolina Botanical Garden
University of North Carolina
Totten Center
Laurel Hill Road
Chapel Hill   27514
919-967-2246

Tyron Palace Restoration
610 Pollock Street
New Bern   28560
919-638-5109

NORTH DAKOTA

International Peace Garden
Dunseith   58329
701-263-4390

OHIO

Krohn Conservatory
950 Eden Park Drive
Cincinnati   45202
513-352-4091

Kingwood Center
900 Park Avenue West
Mansfield   44906
419-522-0211

Stan Hywet Hall and Gardens
714 North Portage Path
Akron   44303
216-836-5533

OKLAHOMA

Will Rogers Horticultural Garden
3500 N.W. 36th Street
Oklahoma City   73112
405-943-3977

Philbrook Art Center
2727 South Rockford Road
Tulsa   71114
918-749-7941

OREGON

Japanese Gardens
Washington Park
Kingston Avenue
Portland   97208
503-223-1321

International Rose Test Garden
Washington Park
400 S.W. Kingston Street
Portland   97201
503-248-4302

PENNSYLVANIA

Phipps Conservatory
Schenley Park
Pittsburgh   15213
412-255-2376

Swiss Pines
Charleston Road
Malvern   19355
215-933-6916

Longwood Gardens
Route 1
(P.O. Box 501)
Kennett Square   19348
215-388-6741

Morris Arboretum
9414 Meadowbrook Avenue
Chestnut Hill
Philadelphia   19118
215-247-5777

RHODE ISLAND

Green Animals
380 Cory's Lane
Portsmouth   02871
401-683-1267

Wilcox Park
17½ High Street
Westerly   02891
401-348-8362

SOUTH CAROLINA

Brookgreen Gardens
Route 17 South
Murrells Inlet   29576
803-237-4218

Magnolia Plantation
Ashley River Road
Charleston   29407
803-571-1266

Middleton Place
Ashley River Road
Charleston   29407
803-556-6020

SOUTH DAKOTA

McCory Gardens
South Dakota State University
6th and 27th Streets
(Box 2207–C)
Brookings   57007
605-688-5136

TENNESSEE

Memphis Botanic Garden
750 Cherry Road
Memphis   38117
901-685-1566

Dixon Gallery and Gardens
4339 Park Avenue
Memphis   38117
901-761-2409

Tennessee Botanical Gardens
Cheekwood
Forrest Park Drive
Nashville   37205
615-352-5310

TEXAS

Fort Worth Botanic Garden
3220 Botanic Garden Drive
Fort Worth   76107
817-870-7686

Dallas Civic Garden Center
State Fair Grounds
(P.O. Box 26194)
Dallas   75226
214-428-7476

Dallas Arboretum and Botanical Garden
8617 Garland Road
Dallas   75218
214-327-8263

Bayou Bend Gardens
1 Westcott Street
(P.O. Box 130157)
Houston   77219
713-529-8773

UTAH

State Arboretum
University of Utah
Building 436
Salt Lake City   84112
801-581-5322

Utah Botanical Gardens
1817 North Main Street
Farmington   84025
801-451-3204

VERMONT

Shelburne Museum
Route 7
Shelburne   05482
802-985-3344

VIRGINIA

Monticello
Route 53
(P.O. Box 316)
Charlottesville   22902
804-295-8181

Colonial Williamsburg
(P.O. Box Drawer C)
Williamsburg   23187
804-229-1000

Norfolk Botanical Gardens
Airport Road
Norfolk   23518
804-853-6972

WASHINGTON

Rhododendron Species Foundation
Route 18
(P.O. Box 3798)
Federal Way   98063
206-927-6960

Washington Park Arboretum
Japanese Tea Garden
University of Washington
East Madison and Lake Washington Boulevard East
Seattle   95195
206-543-8800

Woodland Park
Rose Garden
5500 Phinney Avenue
Seattle   98103
206-782-1265

WEST VIRGINIA

Sunrise Garden Center
746 Myrtle Road
Charleston   25314
304-344-8035

WISCONSIN

Paine Art Center and Arboretum
1410 Algoma Boulevard
Oshkosh   54901
414-235-4530

Mitchell Park Horticultural Conservatory
524 South Layton Boulevard
Milwaukee   53215
414-278-4383

WYOMING

Cheyenne Botanical Garden
710 South Lions Park Drive
Cheyenne   82001
307-637-6458

Index

Arcadia, California 52–57
Atlanta Botanical Garden 132–135
Atlanta, Georgia 132–135

Balboa Park 66–71
Beverly Hills, California 32–35
Bliss, Mr. and Mrs. Robert 12, 155
Boddy, E. Manchester 49
Boston, Massachusetts 8, 214–217
Bourn, Mr. and Mrs. William II 23
Britton, Nathaniel Lord 195
Burnham, Daniel 9
Brooklyn Botanic Garden 13, 188–193

California 22–73
Callaway, Cason and Virginia 11, 12, 129
Callaway Gardens 11, 128–131
Central Park, New York 8
Charleston, South Carolina 136–147
Charlottesville, Virginia 148–153
Chicago, Illinois 8, 9, 11, 98–103
Chicago Botanic Garden 13, 92–97
Chicago Park District 98–103
City Park 110–113
Cloisters, The 13, 184–187
Columbus Park, Chicago 11

Dallas, Texas 74–85
Dallas Arboretum and Botanical Garden 10, 11, 13, 74–85
Deering, James 10, 115
Delaware 162–173
Descanso Gardens 13, 48–51
Downing, Andrew Jackson 8
Drayton family 137
Dumbarton Oaks 10, 11, 12, 154–161
Du Pont, Alfred I. 169; Alfred Victor 169; Henry Frances 163; Pierre 10, 11, 175
Du Pont de Nemours, Eveline Gabrielle 163

Encinitas, California 72, 73

Fairchild Tropical Garden 12, 120–123
Farrand, Beatrice 10, 155
Filoli 10, 22–27
Florida 114–127

Fort Worth Botanic Garden 12, 86–91
Fort Worth, Texas 86–91
Four Arts Garden 124–127
Freer, James 10
Fuller, Henry B. 10

Gardner, Isabella Stewart, Museum 13, 214–217
Garfield Park 11, 100, 101
Georgia 128–135
Getty, J. Paul 43
Getty, J. Paul, Museum 13, 42–47
Glencoe, Chicago 92–97
Grant Park 102, 103
Greenleaf, James 10

Hare and Hare 12
Hare, Herbert 12
Hearst Castle 28–31
Hearst, William Randolph 10, 12, 29
Hertrich, William 59
Hoffman, F. Burrall 115
Huntington, Henry Edwards 59
Huntington, The 10, 58–65

Iida, Juki 21
Illinois 92–103

Jackson Park, Chicago 9
Jefferson, Thomas 7, 8, 149
Jekyll, Gertrude 13
Jensen, Jens 11, 101

Kennett Square, Pennsylvania 174–183

La Canada, California 48–51
Larabee, Ruth Baird 73
Le Nôtre, André 143, 169, 175
Lincoln Park 9, 98, 99
Long Island, New York 206–213
Longue Vue 11, 104–109
Longwood Gardens 10, 11, 174–183
Los Angeles State and County Arboretum 13, 52–57
Louisiana 104–113

McHarg, Ian 13
Magnolia Plantation 136–141
Malibu, California 42–47
Massachusetts 214–217
Miami, Florida 114–123
Middleton, Henry 8, 143; William 143
Middleton Place 7, 8, 9, 142–147
Montgomery, Robert 121
Monticello 7, 8, 148–153
Morgan, J. P. 10
Morgan, Julia 29

Nemours 10, 168–173
New Orleans, Louisiana 104–113
New York 184–213
New York Botanical Garden 13, 194–199
New York, New York 8, 184–205

Old Westbury Gardens 9, 10, 13, 206–213
Olmsted Brothers 8, 17, 21
Olmsted, Frederick Law 8, 9

Palm Beach, Florida 124–127
Peirce family 175
Pennsylvania 174–183
Perkins, George Walbridge 201
Phinney, Guy 17
Phipps, John 207
Pine Mountain, Georgia 128–131
Platt, Charles 10

Quail Botanical Gardens 13, 72, 73

Robinson, Harry and Virginia 33
Robinson, Virginia, Gardens 10, 14, 32–35
Robinson, William 13

San Diego, California 66–71
San Marino, California 59–65
San Simeon, California 10, 28–31
Santa Barbara Botanic Garden 13, 36–41
Santa Barbara, California 36–41
Seattle, Washington 16–21
Sessions, Kate 67
Shiota, Takeo 189
Simms 7, 8

Smithson, Robert 13
South Carolina 7, 136–147
Stern, Edgar B. and Edith Rosenwald 105
Suarez, Diego 115

Texas 74–91

University of Washington Arboretum 12

Virginia 7, 148–153
Vizcaya 9, 10, 11, 114–119

Washington 16–21
Washington, D.C. 10, 154–161
Washington Park Arboretum 20–21
Washington Park, Chicago 9
Wave Hill 10, 200–205
Wilmington, Delaware 168–173
Winterthur 10, 162–167
Winterthur, Delaware 162–167
Woodland Park, Rose Garden 16–19
Woodside, California 22–27